HOW TO
SELL
YOUR
BUSINESS

And Get The Best Price For It

by
John E. Sampson

ISBN 1-59298-000-7

Library of Congress Catalog Number: 2003100676

Book design and typesetting: Mori Studio

Printed in the United States of America

First Printing: 2003

07 06 05 04 03   6 5 4 3 2 1

Beaver's Pond Press, Inc.
Minneapolis, Minnesota 55439
www.BeaversPondPress.com

For ordering information, call Beaver's Pond Press at (952) 829-8818.

*To my wife, Mary Margaret,
and our children, Mark and Sharon,
who are the greatest joy of my life.*

TABLE

OF

CONTENTS

ACKNOWLEDGEMENTS

No book is possible without the assistance of numerous people. I would like to take this opportunity to acknowledge several of those who have helped me with this book.

First of all, I want to thank Ann Sinclair, former chairman and chief executive officer of ShariAnn's Organics, Inc., who inspired me to write this book. After my firm, Sampson Associates Inc., facilitated the sale of ShariAnn's Organics, Ann said:

> What you should do is write a book for entrepreneurs explaining the various steps in the process of selling a business. I was not prepared for the full scope of activities that a sale involves, and I doubt that most other entrepreneurs are either. They need a book to read that will prepare them for what the process of selling a business entails.

So, Ann, here is the book you inspired.

I am especially indebted to my long-time business associate, Gary Friend, for his many contributions. Gary has extensive experience in valuing businesses, and so I was pleased that he consented to provide the initial draft of Chapter Four, "Determining What the Business Is Worth." His comments on the rest of the book were also greatly appreciated.

Likewise I want to thank two partners in the law firm of Faegre & Benson in Minneapolis for their editorial suggestions on Chapter Nine, "Negotiating the Definitive Sale Agreement." Jennifer Mewaldt, with whom I have worked on several transactions involving the purchase and sale of businesses, provided many constructive editorial suggestions on the entire chapter. Her colleague, Paul Moe, gave me excellent suggestions on the section dealing with environmental representations, the area of law in which he focuses. The counsel of both these attorneys was greatly appreciated.

Throughout this project, I received continuous support from my wife, Mary Margaret, who served as my initial editor and critic. I have benefited greatly from the skills she developed as a college English major and her countless constructive suggestions. I am also indebted to my children, Mark and Sharon, for their editorial comments and suggestions, as well as their overall support of the book.

Several people were very helpful in getting the book ready for publication, including Doug Benson, who served ably as my copy editor; Teresa Hudoba, who was my proofreader; Jack Caravela and Jaana Bykonich of Mori Studio, who did the design work for the book and its dust jacket; and Milt Adams who, as my publisher, helped me throughout the entire process.

Finally, I want to thank the numerous entrepreneurs with whom I have worked on business transactions during the last 25 years. Getting to know how you think, the issues that concern you when selling a business, and the problems you encountered have provided me with considerable insight into the subject matter of this book. You have also provided me with lots of stories to share in hopes that others will benefit from knowing about your experiences.

To all of the above and others I did not mention, thanks for your assistance and support. I could not have done it without your input.

John E. Sampson

INTRODUCTION

For nearly 30 years I have helped people buy and sell businesses. For most of that time I was Vice President for Corporate Development of two **Fortune 500** food and agribusiness companies. There I had responsibility for coordinating the process of making acquisitions and selling businesses for these companies. During that time I negotiated some 100 transactions ranging in size from about $1 million to nearly $1 billion.

I dealt with many entrepreneur owners, learning their reasons for selling their firms, their biggest concerns surrounding a sale, and the common errors they made during the selling process. Since 1996 I have headed my own company representing clients around the country in buying and selling businesses. Most of my clients are sellers, and most are entrepreneur owners. So, again I have learned more about them and the problems they face in selling their businesses.

Out of my experiences I decided that I might be able to help some of the millions of entrepreneurs who own companies and may be considering what they should do when the time comes to sell. So, in this book I candidly discuss every aspect of the process of selling a business. I try to address the numerous issues that I have encountered while working with entrepreneur owners, often citing my own experiences with owners to illustrate various points throughout the selling process.

This book is not directed at professionals—business brokers, accountants, tax specialists, and lawyers—who guide clients through the process of selling a business; there are plenty of specialized books for them with far greater depths of information. Rather, this book is intended for those who are not familiar with the general subject of selling companies.

I aim to provide owners with a basic understanding of what's involved in selling a business. This book is meant to take the mystery out of the process of how a firm is sold, and to enable newcomers to the subject to converse knowledgeably with the "experts" whom they encounter in the selling process. And, above all, this book is meant to help owners do a better job of selling their businesses—including making better decisions throughout the selling process and ultimately securing higher prices for their companies.

DETERMINING WHEN IT'S TIME TO SELL

One of the most important steps in selling a business is deciding when it's the right time to sell. There are several factors that can prompt a decision to sell one's business. Over the next few pages I will discuss many of them.

PREPARING TO RETIRE

While retirement used to be associated with turning age 65 and becoming eligible for Social Security and other retirement benefits, this is no longer the case. An increasing number of people want to retire by age 55, and some even earlier, while others continue to work well past age 65 either because they still enjoy it or do so out of necessity. So, retirement is no longer associated primarily with one's age. It is more apt to be associated with one's state of mind (When do you want to leave your business and engage in leisure activities or do volunteer work?), as well as with one's ability to afford to do so financially.

Whatever the case, a business owner has to decide the "right" retirement age for himself. That then leads to the issue of what he does with his business, which will most likely be selling it.

Wanting to do Something Different with Your Life

Some business owners do not necessarily want to retire when they decide to explore the potential of selling their business; they just want to do something different. Some may even want to purchase a business in another field. Depending on the individual's age, the goal might be to pursue a second career—such as getting a law degree, going to graduate school to pursue another vocation, or deciding to run for political office. Regardless of what the motive may be, a change in career paths raises the same issue as retirement: How do I sell my business?

Differences Among Co-Owners

A third reason owners often decide to sell their business comes into play when there is more than one owner and at least one of them no longer wants to remain in the business. It may be because they have different beliefs about the direction the business should go, or because they may no longer have an amicable working relationship, or because one of the owners wants (or needs) to cash out his share of ownership. In many such instances, the remaining owner simply buys the other one out, either with cash up front or paid over time, and the business continues to operate.

Often the owners will have a "buy-sell" agreement in place, which provides that the owner wishing to stay will have the right to buy out the owner wanting to leave, and the agreement will provide for a valuation formula to fix the buyout price. But, sometimes the remaining owner does not have the financial wherewithal to buy out the other owner or simply does not

> **Note:** The male gender is used throughout this book for simplicity. The author means no offense or slight whatsoever to the countless number of successful female entrepreneurs and business owners.

want to (e.g., he may be approaching the time he wants to retire). Then, the owners collectively need to face the issue of how they will sell their business.

CHANGE IN THE OUTLOOK
FOR THE INDUSTRY OR BUSINESS

Another event that frequently induces an owner to seek to sell a business is a changing outlook for either the industry in which the business operates or a changing outlook for the business itself. People generally assume that the kind of change stimulating a sale would be a negative one. And, that can be the case. If a company loses some major customers and sees little probability of regaining the lost sales, it might be better to sell the remaining business for a lower price than it would have originally been worth, rather than try to carry on and suffer from excessive operating costs due to a shrunken critical mass.

Likewise, an entire industry may change and cause an owner to decide to sell—or in some cases postpone the sale—of his company. I had a client whose business derived 75 percent of its sales from foodservice items sold to airlines—including hand-cooked omelets and fancy breakfasts for first-class passengers and sandwiches for those in coach. We were in my office one day talking about the information to include in an offering memorandum we were developing for sale of the company.

It happened to be the morning of September 11, 2001—the day terrorists plowed airplanes into the World Trade Center towers and the Pentagon. That was one time where the nature of the industry and the company's outlook changed just as we were talking. In the short term, airline travel fell sharply, and airlines quickly cut back their foodservice programs. We had to put the sale process on hold to allow the company to re-group and shift sales to allied customers, feeling the value of the company would be better over time than if we proceeded to sell near-term for a reduced price. The company and its value did recover.

But, the outlook for a company or its industry in general may also change for the better and trigger a desire to sell. For example, if a new product is developed that stimulates aggressive sales, it may also spark the need for greatly expanded production facilities, and the owner may not be able (or want) to invest the capital required to optimize the sales potential. The company's value may have increased because of this new product, but the business may need the resources that only a larger firm or new owner with deeper pockets can supply. In such an instance, both the seller and the ultimate buyer could benefit from a sale of the business, with overall value being enhanced in the process.

AVAILABILITY OF A HIGHER THAN NORMAL VALUATION

The sharp run-up in stock prices during the second half of the 1990s resulted in a major increase in price-earnings multiples. While this was especially true for technology companies, nearly all industries saw their multiples jump well above traditional levels. This, in turn, increased the value of most businesses (both publicly traded and privately owned) and created a very attractive environment for selling companies.

As a result, many entrepreneurs decided to take advantage of this opportunity and sell their businesses, realizing prices that were well above what they could have received five years earlier and that represented higher multiples of earnings than may be achieved for some time into the future. They seized the opportunity and capitalized on it. While we may not see such an overall favorable selling environment again for many years, there will always be times when it is more attractive to sell a business than other times, and business owners need to be alert to take advantage of them—if they are harboring any thoughts about a possible sale.

SHARP RUN-UP IN REAL ESTATE VALUE OF A FACILITY'S LOCATION.
One of my clients was interested in purchasing a business in
Denver. The business had an old facility in the warehouse
district just off the downtown area. The property was not worth
much until Denver decided to build a new baseball park—
Coor's Field—within a block of the facility. Suddenly the value
of the property shot upward. The company decided to sell the
property, which in turn created a major capital gain. At the same
time, my client was interested in purchasing the Denver
operation of this firm, which was losing money for its East
Coast owner.

As a result of the great gain the owner received from the sale of
its downtown Denver facility, he became willing to consider a
sale of its Denver operation to my client when he otherwise
probably would not have. My client was willing to purchase the
business without the downtown property because he had space
in his own Denver facility to which he could transfer the target
business. The moral of the story is that, if your real estate has
enhanced value beyond its value to the business, it is worth
considering how best to optimize the value of both the real
estate and the business, often by selling to separate buyers.

**UNUSUALLY HIGH GROWTH IN SALES AND EARNINGS OR IN INDUSTRY
VALUATIONS.** Sometimes businesses experience unusual growth
in sales and earnings, thereby enhancing their value. Other
times, whole industries come into a particularly attractive selling
environment, raising values for companies in those industries
above the standard norm. In such instances, owners of a
business that is blessed by particularly attractive growth or that
is part of an industry experiencing especially good valuations
should give special consideration to a potential sale that would
capitalize on such an environment.

There is an old adage about the right time to sell a business: Sell
when the business has a big "bud" on it, not when it is in "full
bloom." Buyers will pay more when a business, like a flower, is

still growing nicely and they can see there is more attractive growth to come. But if you wait until the business is in full bloom, potential buyers may feel that future growth is uncertain and may want to pay less, even though current earnings are higher than they were when the business was in the "bud" stage. Thus, if you are thinking about a potential sale over the next few years, take advantage of opportunities that may come along when earnings have grown nicely and the outlook still is good, rather than wait too long and risk having the outlook slow down or potentially even decline, as a flower does when it starts to lose its petals.

One family I know built up its business in frozen dough by focusing on croissants. In the late 1980s and early 1990s croissants became extremely popular; the business grew rapidly, and its value mushroomed. I think the family realized that the rate of growth for croissants would not be sustainable, just as it had not been for muffins before nor would it be for bagels later. They decided to sell their business just before it went into full bloom and reaped an extremely high price, one that they probably could not have received just a year or two later. This is another example of the importance of timing in selling a business.

RECEIPT OF AN ATTRACTIVE UNSOLICITED OFFER

Sometimes a business owner will receive a totally unsolicited offer to buy his business. It may be from a competitor who expects to achieve synergistic benefits by putting the two companies together. It may also come from a firm that sees an entrepreneur-owned company filling in geographic territory that it does not yet cover. Or an offer may come from a company that wants to add the target company's product line to its own.

Whatever its source, an unsolicited offer should be carefully considered, especially if the owner has harbored the thought of possibly selling in the not-too-distant future. Among the questions that need to be considered are:

- Is this truly a preemptive offer, or would I likely receive more if I went through a regular selling process?

- Should I counter with a higher price, and if so how much higher?

- Does the firm have the financial wherewithal to pay the price in cash?

- What is the buyer likely to do with my business and with my employees?

- Will the buyer continue to operate my facility, or close it down to gain efficiencies?

In some instances it is best for an owner to sell to the firm making the unsolicited offer. One of my long-time neighbors owned a firm in the electrical supply distribution business, with warehouses spread across the country. One day he invited me to lunch at his country club. He, like most business owners, was interested in what his business was worth, not because he intended to sell it, but to help him in estate planning as well as to satisfy his general curiosity. Knowing that I was in the business of advising firms on buying and selling businesses, he shared some financial information on his company during our luncheon discussion.

After I had reviewed the material briefly, he asked what I thought his business was worth. I gave him a value significantly higher than he had expected. About a year later, another company that had long admired his business approached him with a totally unsolicited offer. After some reflection he decided to sell. Later I learned that the price he received was virtually identical to the estimate that I had given him informally at that luncheon meeting. The price I had ball-parked was based on what I thought he could get in a formal selling process. Since he was able to get that amount through an unsolicited pre-emptive offer, he was wise to take it. In this instance, the old adage "a bird in hand is worth two in the bush" was right.

That is not always the way an unsolicited offer turns out, however. In most instances, people making unsolicited offers are on the low side of what a business would bring in a formal selling process. They usually do not have detailed knowledge of the company when they make such an offer, and most tend to be conservative in what they put on the table. Thus, most owners who receive unsolicited offers would do better to seek advice from a professional on what their business is worth. Assuming owners receive a significantly higher valuation from the professional, they would probably be well advised to sell their businesses through a formal selling process, if they are ready to sell.

Another one of my clients had a very profitable food processing business, with a strong branded regional product position in both the foodservice and retail markets. The two owners received an unsolicited offer, which they rejected after some reflection. Later, they asked my firm to give them an estimated valuation of their business. We came back to them with a valuation analysis that was substantially higher than what they had been offered, and they decided to retain us to undertake a formal selling process. When the sale is completed, I expect the price will be substantially higher than what they were originally offered.

OTHER FACTORS

Sometimes a business grows to a point where it will require a substantial amount of additional capital to finance its continued growth, and the owners do not have the ability to provide it or do not wish to take the required personal risk to supply the needed capital. Another one of my clients operated a fast-growing foodservice distribution business focused on ethnic restaurants. The company had developed a successful concept and added a second warehouse in an adjoining geographical region.

It was apparent that the concept could be rolled out across many more states—perhaps even across the entire country. But, as the company continued to grow, it required ever larger amounts of working capital to support its growth. The principal owner had to personally guarantee bigger and bigger amounts of debt. His entire net worth was tied up in the company. Most estate planners will encourage such entrepreneurs to diversify their investments and reduce their dependence on a single activity, especially if it is heavily leveraged with the prospect of needing even more capital.

There can be numerous other reasons that might prompt an owner of a business to decide to sell at a particular time. A divorce may require an owner to liquefy his assets as part of the settlement. A death may cause the surviving spouse to sell because she does not know how to operate the business, or does not wish to. In addition, children who inherit a business may decide that they would prefer investing their time, energy, and money in something other than their parents' business.

INSTANCES WHEN A FORMAL SELLING PROCESS MAY NOT BE NECESSARY

After reaching a decision to sell their business for whatever reason, most business owners would benefit from a formal selling process along the lines that will be discussed in this book. There are, however, a few instances when a formal selling process may not be necessary. In the case of an owner receiving a very attractive unsolicited offer, the process of marketing the company can be eliminated, although negotiating a definitive sale agreement and preparing for a closing will still be necessary.

Likewise, some owners have family members whom they have groomed for years to step into their shoes when the time comes. Again, a formal selling process will not be necessary, as there are a variety of ways to transfer ownership to one or more children.

For example, depending on the value of the business, ownership might be gifted over a period of time, giving the children a portion each year.

Or, the children might pay their parents a fixed amount each year to purchase the business, either (1) taking over all ownership initially, making a down payment, and then paying off the balance in the form of a loan over several years (either through a bank loan or a loan from the parents) or (2) buying a specific amount of shares each year until ownership is transferred in full. The selection of an option will be influenced by the value of the business, the parents' need for cash upfront versus receiving payments over time, the children's ability to raise cash initially versus buying the business over time, and the projected tax impact on the individuals involved.

Instead of letting a family member take over ownership of the business, an owner ready to retire might have a plan to sell his business to a long-time associate, either for a one-time cash payment or over time as the new owner earns money from the business. An owner might also desire to sell the business to his employees. This is commonly done through an ESOP (employee stock ownership plan), which enables the employees to gradually purchase a greater percentage of ownership in the business as earnings from the business allow them to until they ultimately purchase all the stock from the owner.

But, in most cases, an owner will not have a predetermined buyer in mind. And, that is when the issue of "How do I sell my business?" comes to the forefront. That is the question I will focus on in the chapters that follow.

THE ROLE OF AN INTERMEDIARY IN SELLING A BUSINESS

After an owner has made the decision to sell his business, the next question is usually how to accomplish the sale. Since most owners are not experienced in the process of selling a business, many decide to engage a professional to assist them. The professional may be a trusted lawyer or the company's accounting firm, if they are experienced in selling businesses. Often, however, a seller will decide to engage the services of an intermediary or business broker. In simplified terms, intermediaries perform the same basic role for a business owner seeking to sell his company that a realtor performs for a homeowner seeking to sell a residence.

FUNCTIONS PERFORMED BY AN INTERMEDIARY

While the range of services varies among intermediaries, the following is a list of services provided by most intermediaries.

HELP THE OWNER PREPARE THE BUSINESS AND ITS PEOPLE FOR A SALE. One of the first and most important steps in selling a business is getting the business and its people ready for a sale.

With respect to getting the business ready for a sale, this may involve improving sales and the business outlook, as well as reducing expenses and enhancing profitability. Preparing employees for the sale will include when, who, how, and what to tell employees. An experienced intermediary can provide an owner good counsel on each of these subjects. Helping the owner better prepare for the sale may allow him ultimately to realize greater value for his business than he might have without such counsel.

ASSESS THE VALUE OF THE BUSINESS. Since many business owners will not have a well-founded knowledge of what their business is worth, an intermediary can help the owner assess the value of the business. An intermediary should use a variety of measures to conduct the financial analyses of the selling company.

One of the most useful of these valuations is a discounted cash flow analysis, which takes projected earnings along with other cash flow items and discounts them back to a present value for the business. Another commonly used technique is to derive a projected valuation by taking a multiple of EBITDA (earnings before interest, taxes, depreciation, and goodwill amortization). In some industries a multiple of dollar sales may also be used to provide a rough valuation. We will delve more deeply into alternative valuation approaches in Chapter Four.

It is entirely appropriate for a business owner to ask an intermediary to provide a preliminary valuation at no charge before he enters into a formal contract with the intermediary. That way, the owner can see if his ideas about a selling price are in line with those of the prospective intermediary.

DEVELOP A LIST OF PROSPECTIVE BUYERS WITH THE SELLER. If the intermediary has completed numerous transactions in the same industry as the selling company, he can bring critical knowledge of potentially good prospects. He can supplement that knowledge by using comprehensive directories put out by industry associations to add the names of additional prospects. The owner undoubtedly will have his own thoughts about who might have an interest in buying his company. Working together, the client and the intermediary should be able to develop an extensive list of prospective buyers.

When I sit down with a client to exchange lists of prospects, I try to have identified 75 to 80 percent of the prospects on his list (without having previously seen his list) and to have the names of at least twice as many prospects on my list as he has on his. I won't have all the names on my client's list because he knows things about his competitors and his industry that I don't. But I should have most of his names on my list, and many others that he does not have. Good research is part of my job; that's one of the things a client pays me to do, and he should expect me to be thorough in developing a comprehensive list of good prospects.

PREPARE AN OFFERING MEMORANDUM WITH THE ASSISTANCE OF THE SELLER. I will discuss much more about how to develop a good offering memorandum a little later, but at this point it is important to note that the offering memorandum is the single most important selling tool in the entire sale process. It should reveal the company's inner soul and convince the reader that this is a very attractive business to purchase.

Thus, a business owner should make sure that any intermediary he retains is skilled in preparing offering memorandums. Ask the intermediaries you interview to let you look through a couple of their old offering memorandums. Confidentiality limitations will likely preclude an intermediary from leaving these documents with you, but you can get a good idea of their completeness by leafing through them during the meeting.

CONTACT PROSPECTIVE BUYERS APPROVED BY THE SELLER. Once the list of prospective buyers and the offering memorandum are completed, the intermediary should begin calling the prospects. The intermediary should contact directly a key decision-maker in each prospective company. Depending on the company's size, that may be the owner, the CEO, or (in a large firm) the vice president for corporate development.

When the intermediary calls, he should offer to fax a summary of the seller's business, which I try to keep to two tightly written pages. The summary should provide a good overview of the business and why it is an exciting opportunity—without identifying the name of the company. The intermediary should also be persistent in following up with prospects until he gets a definitive expression of interest—or lack thereof—from each one.

GET A CONFIDENTIALITY AGREEMENT SIGNED BY BOTH PARTIES. It is standard to ask an interested party to sign a confidentiality agreement (a three-year term is common), which will protect the signer from using the information he receives to the detriment of the selling company. Once the interested party indicates a willingness to sign the confidentiality agreement, the name of the selling party has to be revealed, as its name will be in the confidentiality agreement. An intermediary usually will ask the interested party to sign the agreement and fax it back to him, whereupon he will have it countersigned by the company owner.

PROVIDE COPIES OF THE OFFERING MEMORANDUM TO PROSPECTS. After receiving the signed confidentiality agreement, the intermediary should provide the interested party with a copy of the offering memorandum. If at any time an interested party who has received a copy of the offering memorandum drops out of the process or is not a successful bidder, the intermediary should request the return of the offering memorandum. Alternatively, he may ask for a letter from that company attesting that the offering memorandum and any copies of it have been destroyed. This is important so that the seller can provide the ultimate buyer with reassurance that no other party still has confidential information about the company gained during the selling process.

SEEK PRELIMINARY VALUATIONS FROM INTERESTED PARTIES. After they have had about three weeks to review the offering memorandum, prospects who remain interested should be asked by the intermediary to provide a preliminary valuation of the business. This will be non-binding and may even be in the form of a valuation range. The purpose of getting preliminary valuations is to determine which four to six companies have the greatest interest in the business (as measured by price). These companies will be invited to meet with the owner and his senior management team, and they will also be provided with additional confidential information beyond that contained in the offering memorandum.

ARRANGE MEETINGS BETWEEN INTERESTED PARTIES AND THE SELLER. Once it has been decided which firms to invite into the next round of the process, the intermediary should work with the seller and each of the prospects to set up separate meetings with each party. Such meetings will usually begin with the seller and his senior management team making presentations about their business, with each entertaining questions from the prospective buyer. Questions will be based on the information in the offering memorandum, the material covered in the oral presentations, and other issues that the prospective buyer may have about the business. Typically, these meetings last about three hours.

The rest of the day is often turned over to meetings among the respective disciplines (e.g., the finance people representing the seller and the potential buyer meet together), as well as a review of the additional confidential material that the selling company is making available. These meetings give prospective buyers an opportunity to get to know the senior management of the selling firm, as well as to gain substantial additional information on the company. They constitute a key component of a prospective buyer's due diligence efforts and provide the basis of information used in making the formal purchase offers.

HELP THE SELLER PREPARE FOR MEETINGS WITH PROSPECTIVE BUYERS. Considerable planning is needed if the meetings with prospective buyers are to be successful in conveying a positive message about the selling company. Each executive will need a script for his oral remarks, and all presentations should be well rehearsed. Materials for the due diligence reviews that follow the formal presentations also have to be prepared. An intermediary with extensive experience in such meetings can be an invaluable resource to a seller in the preparation process, and sellers should rely heavily on such a person to help them prepare for these due diligence meetings.

SEEK FINAL BIDS. About three or four weeks after the due diligence meetings are completed, the intermediary should receive formal bids from the prospects. This should be preceded by the intermediary sending a letter of instructions to the interested parties, providing the due date for the bids, indicating what should be covered in the final offer letters, and detailing to whom the letters should be sent.

During the week before the bids are due, the intermediary should call all the prospects to see if they have any final questions that will have to be addressed and to make sure they will get their final bids in on time. Such calls may also be used to try to stimulate the prospects to provide as high a valuation as possible because of the competitive nature of the bidding process (e.g., "There can be only one winner, so you might want to think about increasing your bid an extra 5 or 10 percent to enhance your chances of being that winner").

If a prospect does not get its bid in by the deadline, the intermediary should call to find out why the bid was not received. The bid may have been sent to the wrong address or fax number; the company may need an extra day or two because of an unexpected problem; or the company may have decided on the last day not to make a bid. Whatever the reason the bid was not received, the intermediary needs to find out what it was and convey the reason to the owner.

HELP THE SELLER ASSESS ALTERNATIVE BIDS AND TRY TO GET THEM SWEETENED. Once the bids are received, the intermediary needs to review them with his client. Assuming there are at least three or four solid bids, I find it helpful to make a table for my client that summarizes the key components of each bid so that the options can be compared easily. Whatever the level of bids, it is usually worth going back to the top two or three parties to seek sweetened terms.

You can, of course, go back and seek a higher dollar amount, but there may be other items that a seller would like to address before making a final decision on which prospective buyer to accept. I have seen treatment of the seller's management team become a key determining factor, with a firm other than the highest bidder ultimately getting the nod. Throughout this process of determining the final buyer, the intermediary can provide a valuable service in helping the seller get the best terms he can from the buyer he prefers most.

COORDINATE NEGOTIATIONS, INCLUDING THE DEFINITIVE SALE AGREEMENT. Once oral agreement has been reached on the basic terms for the sale, work turns to development of the written agreements. The formal definitive sale or purchase agreement may be preceded by a non-binding letter of intent, which ethically commits both the buyer and seller to the basic terms and provides a "good faith" understanding between the parties.

As work proceeds on the legal documents, there will be continued negotiations on a wide variety of business and legal issues. Assuming the seller wants him to, the intermediary can coordinate the overall process. He can also serve as an important conduit for resolving various business issues between the parties, thereby allowing the seller to stay out of the middle of the foray.

Generally, the lawyers will have to resolve any legal issues themselves, but even here the intermediary can make sure they are communicating at important times. He may even be part of the discussions between the lawyers if a business counterpart from the other side is also involved. Keep in mind that, in the final analysis, lawyers usually resolve legal issues based on the direction they receive from their clients. Having the intermediary be a part of the legal discussions can enhance the probability that the seller's lawyer follows the direction given to him by the seller.

HELP THE SELLER THROUGH THE DUE DILIGENCE PROCESS. While the legal documents are being prepared and negotiated, it is customary for the buyer to undertake its final due diligence examination of the selling company. This is when the buyer usually asks the seller for more detailed information, including customer lists and tax returns (if not previously provided). An intermediary can assist the seller in deciding how to respond to these requests.

If, for example, the buyer wants to contact key customers to ascertain that they do not have plans to reduce near-term purchases, I will advise a client to ask the buyer to wait until the definitive sale agreement has been agreed to but not yet signed, thereby minimizing the chances that the transaction will not be completed after such contacts are made. Then I usually insist that the seller be a part of these customer contacts to ensure the buyer does not say something inappropriate. The buyer can still back out because the binding contract has not been signed, but unless he finds something totally unexpected during these customer contacts, the buyer is not likely to walk—he is too committed by the time negotiations on the definitive contract have been completed.

HELP THE SELLER PREPARE FOR THE CLOSING. As the closing date approaches, the intermediary can help the seller make final decisions. Often the buyer will want to issue a press release, and the intermediary can help the seller edit the buyer's draft. The final purchase price may have to be computed based on the purchase agreement, and instructions will need to be issued for wiring the funds. The intermediary can help the seller make sure that appropriate information is provided and assure the seller that the process is drawing to a proper close.

WHAT YOU SHOULD EXPECT TO PAY AN INTERMEDIARY

Most intermediaries will seek a retainer, paid either up front or over time, to cover their initial efforts working on a given transaction. For most smaller or medium-sized businesses, this commonly ranges from $5,000 to $10,000 per month. Other intermediaries will charge an hourly fee. Depending on the area of the country, this is typically in the area of $150 to $250 per hour. Part or all of the retainer or consulting fees paid may be subtracted from a success fee.

Besides the retainer or hourly consulting fee, the intermediary will receive a success fee, payable only if the sale closes and the seller collects the proceeds. The most widely used success fee structure for intermediaries—for both acquisitions and divestitures—is the "Lehman's Formula." Under it, the intermediary is paid 5 percent of the first million dollars of transaction value (which includes the value of any interest-bearing debt assumed by the buyer), plus 4 percent of the second million dollars, plus 3 percent of the third million dollars, plus 2 percent of the fourth million dollars, plus 1 percent of the remaining amount of transaction value over $4 million. For a $10 million transaction, the total fee would be $200,000, or 2 percent of the transaction value.

Some intermediaries use a sweetened Lehman's Formula of 6 percent of the first million dollars of transaction value, 5 percent of the second million dollars, and so on. On the other hand, fees are usually about 1 percent of the total transaction value on larger deals, say of over $100 million. Lower fees might also be negotiated if the seller needs or wants fewer services from the intermediary. For example, if the business owner has already been contacted by a prospective buyer who is willing to make a pre-emptive offer, then the intermediary does not have to prepare an offering memorandum or contact a full complement of prospective buyers, and the fee might be reduced accordingly.

A business owner should openly negotiate the fee paid to an intermediary. It is important to the overall partnership between the company and its intermediary that they reach a comfortable agreement on fees. A company does not want to overpay an intermediary, but it needs to pay enough so the intermediary feels good about giving the full level of service that the engaging company expects to receive. If the intermediary is not comfortable with his fee, his service level is likely to fall, and the net result may disappoint both parties.

Keep in mind that a 1 or 2 percent fee is small in relation to the overall transaction value, particularly if the intermediary helps the owner raise the price received for his company by 10 or 15 percent. A good intermediary should be able to negotiate a higher price than a seller might otherwise receive for the business. In most cases, the higher price will cover the intermediary's fee many times over.

DECIDING WHETHER TO USE AN INTERMEDIARY

During my career in the food industry, I personally wrestled numerous times with the question of when to use an intermediary. During the 20 years I served as the Vice President of Corporate Planning and Development at two **Fortune 500** food companies, I leaned toward doing as many deals on our own as possible. Keep in mind that we had a staff of in-house lawyers, skilled financial people, and specialists in other important disciplines such as human relations to work with the corporate development people in my department. But, even with these in-house experts, I always recognized that for many transactions an intermediary was desirable.

In 1996, I formed my own firm to help other companies make acquisitions and divestitures. Now, of course, I generally try to convince potential clients that they should use an intermediary whenever they are going to buy or sell a business. So, I have been on both sides of the issue. Below I have listed instances when I would use an intermediary and other instances when I feel the use of one may not be necessary.

TIMES WHEN AN INTERMEDIARY MAY NOT BE NECESSARY.

1. **When you have a thorough understanding of the process of selling a company.** Some business owners have bought and sold several companies during their careers and have gained extensive knowledge of the buying and selling process. If they are good at it and know how to optimize value whether buying or selling, they may not need a specialist to assist them.

2. **When you have a good outside accountant or lawyer who has negotiated several similar sales and can advise you on all phases of the selling process.** I know business owners who have entrusted the selling process to their attorney or a valued accountant. In most such cases they had long worked with the chosen lawyer or accountant, or they had retained someone on the basis of recommendations from others. If an owner has a predetermined buyer in mind and is satisfied that the prospective buyer has made or will make an acceptable preemptive offer, then he might feel comfortable in turning the process over to his designated lawyer or accountant.

I would, however, raise a concern about relying only on a lawyer or an accountant in a full-blown selling process, because most are not well versed in all phases of selling a business. Generally, they are not experienced in helping a seller prepare an offering memorandum, developing a comprehensive list of prospective buyers, or in calling and following up on an extensive list of prospective buyers. While both lawyers and accountants can play an important role in selling a business, they usually help a seller most when they are part of a team that also includes an intermediary who can coordinate the overall selling process.

Times When an Intermediary Would Be Desirable.

1. **When the seller is not familiar with selling a company and needs a professional to coordinate the entire process.** When my car does not start, I call a specialist to diagnose the problem because I do not know that much about the mechanical workings of an automobile. Similarly, when I have a health or dental problem, I seek the skill of a doctor or dentist to treat the problem because I do not have professional training and experience in these specialized areas. And, when a water pipe springs a leak, I call on the expertise of a plumber to fix it. Likewise, when business owners decide to sell, most are well advised to retain the services of someone whose primary specialty is helping others buy and sell businesses.

As a specialist in selling businesses, the intermediary can guide an owner through the entire selling process and provide objective counsel on each aspect as the process proceeds. This should minimize missteps by the owner at various points along the way, increase the probability of completing a successful sale, and ultimately realize a higher price than would be likely without using an intermediary.

This does not mean an owner should turn all aspects of the selling process over to an intermediary and sit on the sidelines. An owner should constructively interact with the intermediary in all phases of the process. This includes raising questions to gain an understanding of "what," "why," and "how" the intermediary plans to proceed. Most business owners have a good, common-sense feel for business issues and can provide a good check on how their intermediary is proceeding. Likewise, most intermediaries desire an on-going close working relationship with a client and want to keep him informed of their plans as they proceed. Most intermediaries also want to use the client as a sounding board about the list of prospects to be contacted, the content of the offering memorandum, and the proposed terms of the sale.

2. **<u>When it is best for a third party to contact prospects.</u>** Most owners are not the best persons to make cold calls to prospective buyers of their businesses. In some instances the best buyers might be long-time competitors. Also, if the owner calls prospective buyers on his own behalf, he is immediately signaling the name of the company for sale, thereby making control of confidentiality more difficult. Most owners do not want it known in the marketplace that they are pursuing a sale, because a competitor's sales force can use such information to the selling company's detriment with customers. For example, a competitor's salesman might say: "Company A is for sale and may go out of business; you do not want to be faced with supply uncertainty by buying from it."

As an intermediary, I do not disclose the name of my client, the selling company, to a prospective buyer unless or until a senior executive of that firm tells me that the firm is sufficiently interested that it will sign a confidentiality agreement. And then, if my client is particularly concerned about confidentiality, I will explain the concern to the executive and ask that he not discuss the subject with anyone in his organization who will not be directly involved in the evaluation process. This usually causes him to refrain from sharing with his sales force that my client's company is for sale.

As the process proceeds, it also is usually best to minimize contacts between prospective buyers and the seller, except in due diligence and other similar meetings that require the owner's participation. This enables the business owner to wear a "white hat," while the intermediary is charged with communicating the sensitive messages to the prospective buyer, such as key issues in the negotiations.

3. **When the intermediary is a specialist in the seller's industry.** When the intermediary has done numerous transactions in the same industry as the seller's business (as I have in the food industry), it can be a real advantage to the seller. The intermediary then has solid knowledge of who the best prospects are likely to be, often knows key executives in many of the prospective companies, and knows how transactions in the industry are being "priced." This special industry knowledge can be of considerable value to a seller in seeking to maximize the price received for his company.

If you do decide to use an intermediary, meet with three or four different ones and make sure you are comfortable with the one you select. Ask them for the names of other business owners for whom they have sold companies. Ask them to provide you with a no-cost valuation of your business, and ask how they arrived at the projected value. Have them show you examples of offering memorandums they have prepared for other businesses. Above all, make sure that you are comfortable that the intermediary you select will be a true partner in the selling process; you want to feel that he will be your foremost confidant as the process evolves.

PREPARING A BUSINESS AND ITS PEOPLE FOR A SALE

In addition to deciding whether to engage the services of an intermediary, one of the first things an owner needs to do after deciding to sell his business is to get the business and its people ready for a sale. I discussed the role of an intermediary first because his services may be helpful to the owner during this initial step in the selling process.

IMPROVING SALES AND THE BUSINESS OUTLOOK

If an owner has one or more years to prepare a business for sale before placing it on the market, it may be worth trying to enhance sales as much as possible without incurring excessive costs to do so. Typically, a higher growth rate in sales will bring a higher multiple of earnings and thus a greater overall selling price. Perhaps some previously lost accounts can be regained with renewed effort. New accounts might be obtained by adding an additional salesperson who can bring accounts with him. Additional accounts might also be gained by moving into areas adjacent to existing sales territory. And, sales to existing customers might be increased by trying to get them to take on added products or services that a company offers.

The key here is to try to increase sales as much as possible before offering the company for sale—without increasing costs proportionately. If the cost of new sales is proportionately higher than that of existing sales, margins will fall, and the overall effort will probably not enhance the ultimate selling price. But, if one can increase sales and spread fixed costs over more volume, margins will increase, and the corresponding selling price should rise.

Likewise, it is important to try to boost the outlook for sales beyond the current period. Being able to show prospective buyers how they can increase sales after a closing can also increase the selling price, even if historical sales have not grown as fast as the projections for the future. I had two clients in the food industry who owned a very profitable business making fresh tomato products. Sales were growing about 5 percent annually, in line with the industry, but each year the two owners were taking out a very sizeable amount of cash.

The owners had decided that, since they were approaching retirement, they did not want to take on the responsibility of pursuing a major growth strategy. Yet, when they decided to sell their business, my company helped them put together a plan to show potential owners how the sales of the company could be more than doubled within three years if the company's facility was operated year-round instead of only four months annually during the fresh packing season. This could be done by using tomato concentrate in the other eight months for an entirely new line of complementary products. With this knowledge, prospective buyers could readily envision how the company could become much larger, with higher profits, and without needing to make a significant capital investment.

REDUCING EXPENSES AND ENHANCING PROFITABILITY

At the same time an owner is seeking to boost sales (or developing a plan to accomplish this), he should be looking for ways to enhance the profit and loss statement prior to a sale. In particular, the owner should seek to reduce expenses wherever practical. It is usually not wise to cut things that a prospective buyer knows will hurt future sales or will have to be restored after a sale. An owner who does things like eliminating the annual audit (as one of my clients did right before deciding to sell the company), or reducing advertising to a level that will reduce future sales is unlikely to enhance the selling price; it may even hurt the price by causing a buyer to overly revise downward current earnings and earnings prospects.

But, in the year or two before a sale, it is prudent for the owner to go over each expense item, see if any "fat" can be found, and weigh how reductions might be accomplished without cutting into the muscle of the company. Each business is different, but it might be worth looking at several areas. For example:

- Could office operations be tightened up?

- Could any positions in the organization be consolidated?

- Is anyone not carrying his full weight, or not being as productive as the rest of the team?

- Could purchases be made any more efficiently, or other suppliers be given an opportunity to provide lower bids?

- Could any discretionary maintenance be deferred for another year?

Likewise, there may be capital spending items that could be deferred. You could still discuss opportunities for capital spending with prospective buyers so they could see good payback opportunities. But by not taking advantage of them yourself, you can conserve near-term cash and save on depreciation expense.

The overall intent of this exercise is to see if there are ways to reduce unnecessary expenses and enhance earnings. Keep in mind that each dollar of earnings brought to the bottom line is worth a multiple of those same earnings in the form of a higher selling price. So, it's really worth taking a close look at whether, and if so how, the bottom line might be enhanced prior to placing the business on the market. I am not stating that there is a set formula to ensure that each company's sales and earnings, and in turn its selling price, can be boosted. Rather, I am saying that it is worth giving appropriate consideration to this possibility if there is time to do so before undertaking a sale.

Before leaving this subject, it is worth commenting on those situations in which a business is losing money, the outlook for the business is not particularly good, and the owner either does not have a sound strategy in place for turning the company around or does not know how to develop a turnaround strategy. In such situations, it may be worth contacting a turnaround consultant. Such individuals and firms should be willing to review the business and provide the owner with an evaluation of how he would go about reversing the direction of the company's profitability, how long it might take, the likely improvement that might be realized, and the projected cost of such an effort.

Depending on the turnaround consultant's conclusions, it might well be worthwhile for an owner to postpone a sale while he retains such a consultant to help him try to reverse the company's slide. Depending on the nature of the problems and their severity, it could take a year or more to reverse them. The process often involves placing a consultant in the business on a full-time basis for six months or longer. It will not be cheap, but if the effort results in a significant improvement in profitability, the salability of the business—and the ultimate price received—might be greatly enhanced.

PREPARING EMPLOYEES FOR AND
HANDLING THEM DURING THE SELLING PROCESS

One of the important things that a prospective buyer usually wants in a company that it purchases is to inherit a team of good managers who will remain with the business after the closing. That starts with the owner, whom most buyers would like to be available for at least a few months after the sale to assist with the transition. But most buyers know that the owner is unlikely to stay a long time after the sale, and most buyers do not want the former owner to stay for a prolonged period after the closing anyway, being afraid he will interfere with the ongoing operation of the business.

More important to most buyers than the owner staying on for an extended time is making sure that the team of managers below the owner stays on—particularly those who are important to keeping the business operating smoothly after the sale. The new owner may put some of its own people in key management spots in the business. For example, it will probably not need a chief financial officer of the caliber the previous owner had because the purchased company's banking function will likely be consolidated with the new owner's at its headquarters.

But, if many of the people who are critical to operating the business leave shortly after the closing, it could significantly reduce the value of the company. Likewise, if they were to leave before the closing, that could greatly jeopardize the company's ability to function well up to the closing and could reduce the price the seller would otherwise receive. Thus, both because the owner needs his key managers to remain until closing and because prospective buyers will want most of them to stay on after the closing, it behooves an owner to do what he can to keep his employees motivated to stay during the selling process.

The process of keeping your employees with you throughout this important period—and beyond—usually begins with communicating with them. In this regard, the four questions most owners ask about discussing a forthcoming sale with their employees are: "Whom should I tell?"; "When should I tell them?"; "How should they be told?"; and "What should I tell them?" Let's talk a little about each of these important questions.

WHICH EMPLOYEES TO TELL. When an owner begins to consider a sale of his business, he usually is well advised not to tell all of his employees. He may first discuss it with his attorney, or his outside accountant, or even a key right-hand executive. He may want to solicit their thoughts on how he might go about undertaking a sale and how much they think the business might be worth.

Once the owner is committed to embarking on a formal selling process, he will need to confide in others, such as the internal accountant who will prepare needed financial information. As each person is brought into the process, the owner must impress upon them the highly confidential nature of the subject. Each person needs to understand that, if word of the project were to slip out into the organization in general and to sales or brokerage personnel in particular, it could put the selling process at considerable risk.

My rule of thumb is to tell only employees whose services will be needed in the selling process, at least until the process is well along. Whenever individuals are asked to do something outside the ordinary that is related to the selling process, it is best to take them into your confidence and level with them about why they are being asked to work on a special project. Otherwise, they will likely confide their suspicions to others and begin to speculate about what may be going on; that can cause real problems in an organization. However, if an employee is told in confidence about the selling process and why he is being brought into it, usually he will respect the trust that has been shown in him and do his best to keep the subject matter confidential.

WHEN TO TELL EMPLOYEES. I have indicated that the time to tell employees about the selling process is when you need to involve them in the process. Of course, that is true only for the small group of employees who will be directly involved in the process. But when should the rest of the employees be told? Often that time comes on the eve of the visits by a few prospective buyers. At that point, the owner may want to tell his employees that the business is going to have some visitors who are considering making an investment to help expand the business. Such an explanation may be termed partial, but not full, disclosure to the employees.

In most cases, however, I encourage the owner to tell his employees right up front—on the eve of facility visits by prospective buyers—that a sale of the business is being considered, and why. I also suggest he state that, in connection with exploring sale options, there will be some visitors from companies that have expressed interest in the business. The reason I favor openness at that time is to minimize rumors about the purpose of visitors walking through the facility.

More important, by the time facility visits occur, the owner will have received preliminary valuations for his business and will have invited in only those firms offering a price that would be acceptable to him—or a price close enough that the owner feels that after a visit there is a good chance of getting the bidder to raise its offer to an acceptable amount. It is, therefore, highly probable that agreement will be reached to sell the business in the near future. And, thus, the risk to the owner of being open with all employees at that time is relatively low. In fact, the owner may even benefit by being open at that time, with his employees appreciating his honesty and being willing to work harder and having better morale than if word of a pending sale leaked out through rumors.

If there are one or more unions in the business, the eve of the first facility visit would probably also be an appropriate time to tell the union representative, who may be one of the selling company's employees, or the union's business agent. This conversation should be carefully planned, as the union representative will immediately want to know the prospects for retaining all current jobs and will want assurance that its current contract will be assumed by the new owner. In all probability, an owner will want to have the person who does his contract negotiating with the union involved in planning what is said, as well as in attendance at the meeting.

Usually it is not appropriate to tell the union representative until the owner is ready to tell all of the rest of the employees (or at least most of them), and then to do it immediately before (like an hour before) the broader employee group is to be told. This prevents the union representative from being caught by surprise after the employees are told about the pending sale. It also minimizes the time he will have to tell employees about it—and to put his own "spin" on it—before they hear it directly from the owner.

HOW TO TELL EMPLOYEES. When the owner is bringing a few individuals into the selling process, he should tell them directly, preferably in his office, one at a time. Or, if there are a few who need to be brought in at the same time, it might be done in a small conference room or in the boardroom. The owner should discuss openly his motives for seeking a buyer, and he should encourage each person in attendance to ask any questions he may have about the selling process. No written communication should be given to any employees at this time, however. There is always the risk that someone could inadvertently see a copy of such a memo and circulate the content to a wider audience.

WHAT TO TELL EMPLOYEES. Honesty and candor are hallmarks of how employees should be told about the sale process. My advice to owners is to say as much as they are comfortable telling. The owner will be comfortable saying more as the selling process evolves and additional employees are brought into the knowledge circle. By the time most or all of the employees are told, perhaps on the eve of the visits by prospective buyers, the owner should have much greater confidence in the likelihood of a successful conclusion to the selling process than he had when he first told the key operating or financial person that he wanted to consider a sale (again, this is because preliminary bids will have been received by this time).

Initially, or after an appropriate period of reflection, employees will have questions. Again, my advice in responding to employee inquiries is always to be truthful. At the same time, an owner is not obligated to tell employees about all that may be going on in the selling process. For example, in response to a question about whether a sale is likely to be accomplished, the owner might say, "While I cannot say with certainty that a sale will take place in the near future, I need to consider various options for the business, including a possible sale, as I approach the time I want to retire."

Do **not** promise employees that the business will only be sold to someone who will guarantee that all employees will retain their current positions indefinitely, or only to someone who will maintain all the company's current employee benefit plans in their current form. An owner can, however, state that one of the factors that will be weighed among prospective buyers is how they will treat present employees. That shows concern for the employees without making promises amidst an uncertain outcome.

WHAT TO DO WHEN WORD LEAKS OUT PREMATURELY. Despite taking reasonable precautions to keep word of the selling process from leaking out, sometimes it still happens. In responding to inquiries from employees not previously told, first ask them what they have heard and from whom. Rumors frequently spring from salesmen in the industry, who are quick to spread anything negative about a competitor and who sometimes start rumors to aid their businesses. In those cases, one may be able to dismiss the information as just talk in the marketplace. Other times, it may be necessary to tell the person more openly about what is going on.

One Sunday night an associate of mine received a call from the two owners of a business that we were seeking to sell. The owners were very concerned because their lead salesperson had just called and said he had heard in the marketplace that the business was for sale. We had no idea where the information came from or whether it was based on knowledge or was just a rumor. We had just completed the offering memorandum and were starting to make contacts in the industry on what we thought was a very confidential basis (not even giving out the name of the company for sale to anyone who did not agree to sign the confidentiality agreement). It might well have been a lucky guess on the part of some company, which then called our clients' salesman; that company also might have called salesmen of other firms as well, trying to see if they could determine who the available company was.

Nevertheless, our advice to our clients was to level with their salesman, telling him that they had decided to contact a few selected firms regarding their potential interest in purchasing the company. He was also told that the process was just starting, and it was too early to say what the outcome of these contacts might be. The salesman was also urged not to worry about his position and that he should feel free to contact either of the owners from time to time if he heard any other rumors or had questions about how the process was progressing. That seemed to calm the salesman, and we proceeded with the selling process without further significant rumors.

If it should become widely known among employees that a selling process is underway when there has not been an announcement, the owner will have to address the issue directly. He should assemble his employees and tell them what he can, probably along the lines of what our clients told their salesman. Rumors about a pending sale can be very unsettling to employees—taking their minds off their work and encouraging some to look for other positions. Thus, it is important to try to be as open as possible when rumors hit and to attempt to calm their worst fears about an immediate loss of jobs. In some situations when rumors hit, it may be worth putting in place special incentives such as "stay bonuses," which we will discuss next.

MAKING SURE KEY EXECUTIVES REMAIN DURING THE SELLING PROCESS

Besides proper communication with employees during the selling process, owners may decide to take other steps, involving monetary incentives, to enhance the probability that their employees will remain throughout the selling process.

USING "STAY" AND "SELLING" BONUSES. One of the best things an employer can do to increase the probability that his key managers will remain with the business and stay motivated during the selling process is to offer them a "stay bonus." This is paid to key persons who remain with the business until the closing. In most cases stay bonuses do not have to be large sums to keep managers motivated, cause them to delay looking for new opportunities, and discourage them from giving serious consideration to overtures from other firms. Usually a few thousand dollars will be sufficient for most positions; stay bonuses for senior executives will range somewhat higher.

If there are one or two managers who are critical to the selling process and who could positively influence prospective buyers on the price they offer, an owner might also consider giving them a "selling bonus." The amount of the selling bonus should be tied to the price ultimately received. In such cases, no bonus should be given unless the price reaches a given level, and then it might be escalated upward as the price received increases.

Let's assume, for example, that an owner, after thoughtful consideration, has concluded that $15 million would be an acceptable price for his business; we'll call that making "par," in golf nomenclature. No selling bonus would be given for just making par, so a selling price of $15 million would not qualify the senior executive for a bonus. But a selling bonus might be paid in the form of 1 percent of the proceeds received between $15 million and $18 million (we'll call that getting a "birdie"). Then, the senior executive might be given an additional 2 percent of the amount by which the price exceeds $18 million but is less than $20 million (an "eagle"). Finally, the owner might pay an additional 5 percent of any proceeds received over $20 million (the equivalent of scoring a "hole in one").

In this case, if the business were to sell for a much higher price than originally anticipated, say $22.5 million, the executive receiving the selling bonus would get a total of $195,000 ($30,000 for the sale value between $15 and $18 million, $40,000 for the amount between $18 and $20 million, and $125,000 for the amount of the sale price above $20 million). This could be an excellent incentive to the executive to work hard in helping the owner get a very good selling price. In the end, however, the owner would have received an extra $7.5 million (before paying the selling bonus), or 50 percent above the original "par" price, and the $195,000 paid as a selling bonus would be only 2.6 percent of the higher proceeds the owner received.

Obviously, not every sale is going to reach a price deemed to be a "hole in one," so an owner may want to adjust the formula so there is a greater payout for a "birdie," for example, than in my illustration. A seller wants to set the "birdie" in such a manner that his key executive will really be motivated to work closely with him to get a superior price for the business. Then, the executive will be rewarded financially, but the owner will also reap a much greater benefit.

I am working with a business owner who has implemented another variation of a selling bonus for a key employee. While the business owner has all of the stock in the business and did not want to dilute his actual ownership position, he did want to motivate his most important employee to help grow the business in the two or three years before putting it up for sale. Thus, the owner created an informal partnership with the executive.

Under its terms, the owner will get 100 percent of the proceeds of the first $12 million received from the sale of the business, which was the estimated value of the business at the time the informal partnership was established. The executive will share equally with the owner in all proceeds received above $12 million. Thus, in the ensuing two years or so, if the executive helps the owner grow the earnings so that the value of the business increases to $16 million, he will receive $2 million, while the owner will receive $14 million. That is one way to truly motivate a person heavily relied on in operating a business to really help maximize the ultimate sale price.

SEEKING BENEFITS FOR YOUR EMPLOYEES FROM PROSPECTIVE BUYERS. Another step that owners can take toward helping their employees during the selling process is to understand how prospective buyers plan to treat the employees after the closing. Employees know that an owner realistically cannot promise to preserve the status quo for each of them following a sale. But, they do have a right to know whether an owner will look out for them as he considers all of the components of a purchase proposal. In this regard, an owner can request that each prospective buyer include details regarding its plans for his employees. While prospective buyers are unlikely to be able to tell the owner what they plan to do with each employee, they should be able to provide insight about their general termination and severance plans and benefit programs.

If a prospective buyer is going to terminate people, an owner should try to negotiate a good severance package for those who will be terminated. For management, it is reasonable to seek up to a month of salary and benefits for each year of service the person has had with you. Senior executives might expect to receive as much as a year of severance pay, depending on their length of service and the size of the buying and selling firms. The amount one can negotiate will be less for hourly workers, such as a week's pay for each year of service. And, the amounts negotiated will usually have to reflect the content of similar programs the buyer has in place within its own organization.

An owner should also make sure that vacation time "earned" and sick leave benefits "accrued" during his period of ownership are paid to employees. And, he should try to get past service with the company recognized when the new owner computes benefits for employees. One of the most aggravating things to long-time employees is to have to start over as of the closing date in counting years of service for determining the number of vacation days to which they are entitled. If they have been getting three or four weeks, it is very humiliating to have to revert to getting only a week or two. The same is true for determining years of service in a company's pension plan. Usually such items are not "deal breakers" with most prospective buyers, but they can go a long way toward enhancing the legacy that an owner leaves in having sought and received fair treatment for his employees.

DETERMINING WHAT THE BUSINESS IS WORTH

A key question that most company owners have when considering a sale is: "What is my company worth?" While the ultimate answer to that question will not be known until after bids have been received for the business and a fixed sale price negotiated, there are several ways that businesses are valued. Understanding these valuation approaches and applying them to a given business should provide a pretty good idea of what the company would probably be worth if it were to be marketed.

This chapter describes three alternative valuation techniques. While these techniques may not provide exactly the same valuation, the various valuations usually are in the same general range. Keep in mind, however, that the valuation for a given business may differ from other similar companies due to characteristics that the business may or may not have. A discounted cash flow valuation, for example, may yield a specific value, but that value may need to be adjusted (1) downward because the fixed assets are not owned and the firm's products are co-packed for it or (2) upward because the firm has particularly strong brand recognition that provides additional intrinsic value.

THE IMPORTANCE OF HISTORICAL
AND PROJECTED GROWTH

The worth of a business to a prospective buyer is a function of many items, including such things as the strength of its management team, its market share, the number of competitors it has, its technological advantages, the ease or difficulty of entry into the industry, its customer diversification, and its image and brand recognition in the marketplace. But, most important, the value of a business is determined by its ability to grow both revenues and profitability, as reflected in the company's historical and projected financial statements.

Having audited financial statements prepared in accordance with generally accepted accounting principles (GAAP) is a very important factor in establishing the credibility of a company's historical growth record. Audited statements will also minimize the likelihood of any purchase price adjustments that might result from inappropriate accounting uncovered during the due diligence process. Ideally, an owner will want to provide potential buyers with financial results of his company for at least the last five years (initially just in summary form) and projections three years into the future, so they can easily see the evolving trends in sales and profitability.

A historical time line of at least five years will provide greater acceptance of the premise that the company is in a growth cycle than would a shorter time line (such as two or three years). If only a couple of years of history are presented to potential buyers, positive results may be viewed as just an aberration and not a long-term trend. A company's historical financial performance becomes the foundation from which one projects the future outlook and financial results for the company. The stronger and more credible the company's history, the more convincing will be its vision of the future. A positive outlook also creates a feeling of opportunity in the eyes of potential buyers, and can significantly enhance the amount they are willing to pay.

Likewise, prospective buyers will also be particularly interested in hearing the owners' views of the company's future growth potential and the resulting impact on profitability for at least three years into the future. This can simply be an extension of a company's annual strategic planning and budgeting process (for those companies with such a process in place). However, many companies do not have a formal planning and budgeting process and may, therefore, need to rely on an intermediary to assist in developing projections.

MODELING FUTURE GROWTH

The key to modeling future financial performance for a company is preparing growth, cost, and capital investment assumptions that can be supported by actual results and industry developments. This involves an in-depth assessment of the business—focusing on factors, both inside and outside the company, that will affect its future. These might include the health of the general economy, the industry's competitive landscape, the company's key competitive strengths or weaknesses within the industry, key trends that will likely have a significant impact on the company's future sales growth and operating costs, and the amount of capital investment (plant, property, and equipment, as well as working capital) necessary to support the company's business plan.

Once completed, this assessment can become the basis for developing a financial model to project the company's future results. Financial projections for the company should be prepared using the same format and level of detail as in the historical financial statements used internally by the company. These can be entered into a computer spreadsheet so that all key assumptions are linked together and can easily be changed to test different growth and cost scenarios. This enables one to conduct a sensitivity analysis, which can show an owner how important a 1 percent change in the growth rate or a 1 percent increase in gross margins, for example, could be to future profitability.

The first and most important step in constructing a financial forecast is to formulate a comprehensive sales strategy for the business. I always tell my clients to make projections of future sales as aggressive as possible, yet still feel comfortable with them. While I want my clients to be aggressive, at the same time they need to truly believe in the forecast and be able to defend it with prospective buyers based on the company's past performance and ongoing developments in the marketplace.

Ideally, the sales forecast should be developed by revenue segment (product lines, market categories, type of customer, or geographical sectors), showing the anticipated sales increase for each segment and the strategies for achieving the projections. Once in place, the sales forecast becomes the main driver for determining the company's profitability and its resulting cash-flow-generating potential. (We will see shortly that projected cash flow is a key factor in valuing a business.)

Next, relationships between sales and costs (based on history and anticipated future changes in these relationships) need to be applied to the sales forecast to project the remaining elements of the company's profit-and-loss statement. Judgments will be required for items such as:

- Changes in selling prices and the likely impact of such price changes on demand for the company's products (price elasticity).

- The impact of greater sales volume on purchasing inputs at lower prices (economies of size).

- Anticipated inflationary increases for key cost components.

- Fixed and variable elements of the company's cost structure.

- Manufacturing run rates and capacities.

- Changes in staffing requirements.

- Additional marketing and selling expenditures to support the projected sales increases.

- Any increase in capital investment required for plant capacity, increased automation, warehousing, and working capital.

The projected financial statements for the company should include:

- A profit and loss statement—showing profitability at the EBITDA level (earnings before interest, taxes, depreciation, and goodwill amortization).

- A schedule of capital expenditures for property, plant, and equipment—highlighting any major projects.

- An abbreviated balance sheet showing any changes in net working capital requirements (accounts receivable plus inventory, less accounts payable and accrued expenses).

This basic cash flow information, coupled with assumptions for income taxes and an acceptable return on investment rate, will enable the preparer to begin determining an appropriate value for the business.

ADDING BACK UNUSUAL ITEMS TO HISTORICAL AND PROJECTED EARNINGS

During the life of a business, events can occur (sometimes planned and sometimes caused by chance or circumstances) that have a one-time impact on a company's earnings but are not directly related to its daily operations. Such items—if large enough—may cause an aberration in reported earnings that significantly distort the true earnings picture of the company's ongoing operations.

For this reason, the company's historical financial results should be restated excluding any unusual one-time items, both negative and positive. Examples of unusual non-recurring items would include litigation expenses; lawsuit settlements; consulting fees for research, marketing, or operations; start-up expenses for a new facility; a gain or loss on the sale of real estate; and investment income.

In addition, company owners typically have compensation programs for themselves and other family members that would be viewed as excessive by prospective buyers when compared to compensation packages for positions of similar responsibility in the marketplace. For example, owners and family members may receive additional compensation (for taxes or other reasons) in the form of inflated salaries, unique bonuses, specially-designed retirement plans, insurance benefits, a company-provided vehicle, country club memberships, housing allowances, and so on.

Such excessive compensation distorts the true earnings potential of the company. It should, therefore, be removed from both historical and projected earnings because the enhanced compensation for owners and family members will either go away—if they are not retained by the buyer—or will be reduced to market levels if they become part of the new company. If they depart, the buyer will bring in replacements as needed at market compensation rates.

DISCOUNTED CASH FLOW ANALYSIS

There are several methods for valuing businesses, but those most frequently used by the financial community are: (1) discounted cash flow, (2) multiple of earnings, and (3) multiple of sales. The most popular of these—and the one most financial analysts believe to be the most theoretically correct—is the discounted cash flow (DCF) analysis. **The theory behind the DCF valuation method is that the worth of a company is equal to the sum of**

its projected operating cash flows, discounted at a rate of return that reflects the risks associated with the investment and the time value of money. Many Wall Street analysts also use DCF analysis to calculate the market value of a company's stock and determine whether the stock is a good buy for their clients' portfolios at its current selling price. And, major corporations use DCF analysis to evaluate proposed capital investments in plant and equipment.

Making a DCF analysis involves four steps:

- Projecting operating cash flows.

- Determining the residual value.

- Determining the desired rate of return, which becomes the discount rate.

- Making the present value calculation.

Each of these steps is summarized in the sections that follow. I do not expect all readers to readily understand each of these steps. If you do not follow parts of the process, don't worry— just make sure you retain an advisor who does. But, I think a walk through the process is worth including here so those who are comfortable with mathematical computations can follow how a DCF analysis is done.

PROJECTING OPERATING CASH FLOWS. The first step in making a DCF analysis involves projecting the company's operating cash flows on an after-tax basis for the next three to five years, as discussed earlier. Table I illustrates operating cash flow projections on a summary level basis.

Some items to note relating to the operating cash flows include:

- The earnings projections before interest and taxes (EBIT) should exclude any above-market sums for owners' compensation, as previously discussed.

- The tax rate should consist of the federal corporate income tax rate plus the applicable state income tax rate.

- Depreciation and amortization are tax-deductible expenses but are non-cash items; as a result they are added back to operating earnings after taxes.

Table I

THE SELLER COMPANY'S FORWARD PROJECTIONS ($ In Thousands)					
	Year 1	Year 2	Year 3	Year 4	Year 5
Sales	$5,000	$5,500	$6,000	$6,600	$7,300
Cost of Sales	-3,500	-3,850	-4,200	-4,600	-5,100
Gross Profit	$1,500	$1,650	$1,800	$2,000	$2,200
Selling & Marketing Expense	-500	-550	-600	-650	-700
General & Administrative Expense	-500	-500	-500	-550	-600
Earnings Before Interest & Taxes (EBIT)	$500	$600	$700	$800	$900
Taxes on EBIT at 40%	-200	-240	-280	-320	-360
Operating Earnings After Taxes	$300	$360	$420	$480	$540
Depreciation & Amortization	+100	+100	+100	+100	+100
Capital Expenditures	-100	-100	-100	-120	-120
Change in Net Working Capital	-50	-60	-70	-60	-70
Operating Cash Flow	$250	$300	$350	$400	$450

DETERMINING THE RESIDUAL VALUE. The second step in conducting a DCF analysis involves determining a residual or market value for the company at the end of the projection period (often after the the fifth year). Obviously, the life of a business and its income-producing capability are much greater—and spread over a longer time—than the projection period. But, because it is difficult to accurately project a company's financial results beyond the next three to five years, other ways of estimating the value for the period beyond five years need to be used. Several options are available for estimating a company's residual value, including:

1. The <u>estimated book value of the stockholders' equity</u>. This amount would then be added to the cash flow stream projected for the next five years, with each year's amount discounted for the corresponding time period. This approach is a very conservative method of valuing a company's cash flow after the fifth year, since it is more of a liquidation value than a value for an ongoing entity.

2. A <u>multiple of earnings</u> based on values received for similar companies that have recently been sold. This multiple would then be taken times the fifth year earnings and added to the cash flow stream projected for the next five years, and then the entire amount discounted for the corresponding time period.

3. <u>Capitalized earnings</u>, which is usually the preferred financial tool used in a DCF analysis.

In using the capitalized earnings alternative, the analyst starts by determining what the company's earnings would be worth if they remained flat after the five-year projection period—the residual value. Flat earnings are used rather than projecting continued growth because, in addition to being very difficult to project out so far, there is a very heavy discount level after the fifth year (usually more than 50 percent), so future growth discounted this much usually has minimal incremental value over flat earnings.

If we apply the capitalized earnings method to the Seller Company shown in Table I, its residual value would be $3.75 million at the end of Year 5. This is calculated as follows: the operating cash flow of $450,000 in Year 5 is divided by the desired after-tax rate of return for this type of investment. For illustrative purposes, the desired after-tax rate of return is assumed to be 12 percent. Thus, we have the following computation: $450,000/.12 = $3,750,000.

DETERMINING THE DESIRED RATE OF RETURN (THE DISCOUNT RATE). The desired after-tax rate of return is used to discount the projected stream of cash flows and the residual value. It is typically determined by four factors in the marketplace:

1. Long-term return on equity. This is based on historical returns achieved by investors in stocks; since 1926 stock returns have averaged about 12 percent (including both capital appreciation and dividends).

2. Long-term interest rates. This is based on historical returns on long-term corporate bonds; over the last 15 years these rates have averaged 8.5 percent (this has to be on an after-tax basis, which is 5.1 percent after tax assuming a 40 percent combined federal and state income tax rate).

3. The percentage of debt financing relative to equity financing used for investments (leverage). A ratio of 30 percent debt and 70 percent equity would not be unusual.

4. The relative degree of risk associated with the investment (the risk/reward tradeoff). It would not be unusual to use a risk factor for an entrepreneur-owned company of 1.25 (or 25 percent more risk than the average for large publicly traded companies).

If the above assumptions are used in our evaluation, a buyer of the Seller Company would seek a desired rate of return of 12 percent. This calculation is shown in Table II.

In the calculation shown in Table II, a return on equity of 12 percent is taken **times** a risk factor of 1.25 **times** 70 percent

Table II

COMPUTING THE DESIRED RATE OF RETURN							
Desired Rate of Return	=	Return on Equity (12%)	x	Risk Factor (1.25)	x	Equity Financing Component (70%)	+	Debt Financing Component (30% x 5.1%)
Desired Rate of Return	=	12% x 1.25 = 15% x 70% = 10.5% + 1.5% = 12%					

equity financing (which equals 10.5 percent, the equity component of the rate of return) **plus** a debt cost of 5.1 percent after tax **times** 30 percent debt financing (this equals 1.5 percent, the debt component of the rate of return) for a total rate of return of 12 percent (10.5 percent for equity and 1.5 percent for debt).

MAKING THE PRESENT VALUE CALCULATION. The final step in preparing a DCF analysis is to make the present value calculations that determine the estimated value for your business. This simply involves adding up the present value amounts of the company's annual cash flow projections, which have been discounted at the desired rate of return as shown in Table III.

In Table III, the cash flow for year six and beyond is shown as $3.75 million. This is the company's residual value (the cumulative value of the company for all years after the fifth year). It is determined by taking the projected operating cash flow in Year 5 ($450,000) and **dividing** it by the desired rate of return of 12 percent. This equals $3.75 million.

The discount rate used in Table III is 12 percent, indicative of a desired rate of return of 12 percent. Each year is discounted further by the same percentage. In essence this means that a dollar today is worth more than a dollar next year or the year after—each year in the future it is worth about 12 percent less than the year before.

Table III

CALCULATING THE PRESENT VALUE FOR THE SELLER COMPANY		
Year	Cash Flow	Present Value Amount (Using a 12% Discount Rate)
1	$250,000	$223,250
2	300,000	239,100
3	350,000	249,200
4	400,000	254,400
5	450,000	255,150
6+	$3,750,000	$2,126,250
		$3,347,350

Based on a desired return on investment of 12 percent and the cash flow projected for Seller Company, the DCF analysis indicates that the value of the stock of this company is approximately $3.35 million (assuming no long-term debt).

Since DCF analysis requires judgments about the future and also about prospective buyers of a company, it is always prudent to perform what is called a sensitivity analysis. In a sensitivity analysis, one develops alternative scenarios for a business by challenging the assumptions used in the cash flow projections. For example, what if sales grow faster or slower than projected, or what if gross margins are slightly higher or lower than the assumption? What is the probability of these events occurring, and what impact would they have on the company's value?

In addition, one can test the discount rate. What would the impact be on the valuation if the return rate used by potential buyers is higher because of greater perceived risk due to a soft economy? The goal of applying sensitivity analysis to a DCF model should be to formulate a set of assumptions that accurately depicts a company's expected operating conditions and financial results—a "most probable" business/financial scenario. This will enable the seller to determine a fair price for his company and have a well-thought-out and highly defensible rationale supporting the targeted selling price when the company is presented to prospective buyers.

MULTIPLE OF EARNINGS ANALYSIS

A second method that is frequently used to arrive at a company's value is the multiple of earnings analysis, or the ratio of a company's projected selling price to its earnings (P/E ratio). This measurement is one that stock investors have used for decades to determine the relative value of a company's stock price based on its earnings. Naturally, P/E ratios vary by industry based on an industry's historical growth and the outlook for its long-term growth. Businesses in high-growth areas (such as the high-technology sector) carry much higher P/E ratios than companies in mature industries such as steel, transportation, and food processing. In addition, companies with strong brand franchises carry higher P/E ratios than those that do not have well-known brands. And, large publicly traded companies generally command higher P/E ratios than smaller, privately held firms in the same industry.

A good intermediary—particularly one who specializes in a particular industry—should know the earnings multiples for companies recently sold in that industry. The most common earnings multiple used by intermediaries is based on EBITDA (earnings before interest, taxes, depreciation, and goodwill amortization). The main reasons for using EBITDA are:

- It states earnings before interest and income taxes. Earnings after interest and taxes can vary by company depending on a company's financial structure (the percentage of debt versus equity) and its tax rate.

- It converts accounting earnings to cash flow earnings by adding back depreciation and amortization (which are both non-cash items).

Earnings multiples are generally calculated based on a company's trailing earnings for the last 12-month period. For example, if the earnings multiples for businesses that recently sold in your industry were in the range of 5–6 times EBITDA, and if the company's EBITDA for the last 12 months was $600,000 (which is the amount projected for the Seller Company for year one), then a realistic value for the company would be $3.0 to $3.6 million. However, if economic conditions in the marketplace for your business or for the economy in general have recently changed, or if your business is significantly different from those that recently sold either because of size, competitive advantages, or other reasons, then arbitrary adjustments will have to be made to the historical earnings multiples to compensate for these factors.

The projected business valuation of $3.0 to $3.6 million (or a mid-point of $3.3 million) that this approach yielded compares closely with the Seller Company's value of $3.35 million produced by the DCF approach. This merely shows that the two different approaches often produce valuations in the same ballpark, even though the valuation arrived at under the DCF approach has been done using a much more sophisticated analysis.

MULTIPLE OF SALES ANALYSIS

A third method for valuing a business is based on a multiple of sales (rather than earnings); it simply uses the ratio of a firm's selling price to its sales. This method is primarily used for non-manufacturing businesses such as distributors, wholesalers, and other service providers that have relatively few hard assets (property, plant, and equipment) and for which sales (or the company's customer list) is the main driving force and as a result is a key determinant of value.

An intermediary specializing in a distribution industry should know the selling price to sales ratios for companies that have recently been sold. Like earnings multiples, sales multiples are generally calculated based on a company's results (in this case sales) for the last 12 months. For example, if the sales multiples for businesses recently sold in your industry were in the range of .35 to .40 times sales, and if your company's sales for the last 12 months were $10 million, then a realistic starting point for valuing your company would be $3.5 to $4.0 million. Again, adjustments to this price would have to be made for changes in economic conditions, business risk, competitive differences, or any other characteristics unique to your business.

Finally, valuations based on either a multiple of earnings or a multiple of sales are not as sophisticated as a valuation based on a discounted cash flow analysis. The latter takes into consideration several factors about a given company—projected growth, for example—that a multiple of earnings or sales does not. Thus, the DCF analysis is usually a more reliable valuation approach, but multiple valuations can still provide a quick estimate of a given firm's value.

ENTERPRISE VALUE VERSUS SHAREHOLDER VALUE

When discussing the value of a business, it is important to understand the difference between "enterprise value" and "shareholder value." Enterprise value is what the stock of a company is worth excluding any interest-bearing debt and any excess liquidity (such as cash reserves or investments in marketable securities). The value developed for a company using a DCF analysis, a multiple of earnings analysis, or a multiple of sales analysis is its enterprise value. For example, the value established for Seller Company in the DCF analysis section was $3.35 million, which would be its enterprise value.

Shareholder value (or proceeds to the owners), on the other hand, is the net value that the owners of the company would receive after deducting from the enterprise value any interest-bearing debt assumed by the buyer, and adding back any excess cash beyond that needed to operate the business on an ongoing basis. If we assume that the Seller Company also had $500,000 of long-term debt and $200,000 in excess cash (that amount not needed for operating the business on an ongoing basis) on its balance sheet, the shareholder value or proceeds would be $3.05 million as shown in Table IV, a net reduction of $300,000 from the enterprise value.

Table IV

SHAREHOLDER VALUE OR PROCEEDS FOR THE SELLER COMPANY	
Enterprise Value—Using a DCF Analysis (Before Financing and Excess Liquidity)	$3,350,000
Interest-Bearing Debt Assumed by Buyer	-500,000
Excess Cash Retained by Seller	+200,000
Shareholder Value	$3,050,000

VALUING REAL ESTATE OWNED BY A SELLER IN A SEPARATE ENTITY

Based on the advice of financial consultants, business owners frequently set up separate entities (such as a subchapter S corporation or a limited liability partnership) for the sole purpose of acquiring the real estate of a business (its land and buildings). The entity holding the real estate, in turn, leases it back to the operating company. The separate entity or real estate holding company is usually owned entirely by the business owner and other family members and is established strictly for financing and tax purposes.

When selling a business that has assets in two separate entities—operations in one company and real estate in another—a decision must be made up front regarding what to do with the real estate so that the business can be properly priced and so there is no misunderstanding about what assets are to be included in the transaction. A seller in this situation has three options: (1) combine the operating company and the real estate holding company in the information contained in the offering memorandum and sell them together, (2) sell the operating company and enter into a lease with the buyer for the real estate, or (3) sell the operating company and the real estate separately to different buyers. The option selected will typically be influenced by the seller's tax issues and whether the real estate has value beyond its worth to the operating company because of location or other value-enhancing reasons.

From my work with companies that have real estate in an entity separate from the operating business, I have found that it is often beneficial to the seller to combine information on both in the offering memorandum. If a seller agrees to have us do this, we will combine the financial results and balance sheet information into consolidated statements.

We have found that buyers will usually pay a higher price for a business when the real estate is folded in than if the operations and the real estate are sold separately. Prospective buyers tend to look at combined earnings and pay a multiple on that, whereas if the real estate is broken out, buyers will often pay just its appraised value. Obviously, if the real estate has a particularly high value, as I discussed earlier in the case of the seller's land near the new Denver baseball stadium, then it will usually be wise to market it separately.

PREPARING
THE OFFERING
MEMORANDUM

The offering memorandum is the most important marketing tool used in the selling process. Thus, it is important that considerable time and effort be devoted to its preparation. If the business owner decides to use the services of an intermediary, the intermediary may assume the primarily responsibility for pulling the appropriate information together and preparing the initial draft for the owner and his team to review. But the owner should be actively involved throughout the entire process of preparing the offering memorandum to assure that it accurately and appropriately tells the story of his company.

WHAT ITEMS SHOULD BE COVERED?

While the length and format of an offering memorandum will vary among different companies, most will be 30 to 40 pages in length and will contain the following basic items.

AN EXECUTIVE OVERVIEW. The offering memorandum usually begins with an executive summary that provides an overview of the company and of the document itself. The offering memorandums that my firm prepares have an executive summary that starts with a two-page company overview; it includes a brief background on when the company was founded, a general description of its primary products or services, and a summary discussion of its historical and future growth prospects. This is intended to provide enough information to give the reader a sense of what the company does and its future outlook.

The company overview is followed with what I feel is the most important part of the offering memorandum, the section on **key investment considerations**. This summarizes, usually in about two pages, the five to seven most important strengths of the company and the reasons another firm or financial investor should be interested in the available company. These may include such things as strong historical and projected sales and earnings growth, a high market share, an excellent brand name, an attractive production facility, and an experienced management team willing to remain with the business. The key investment conclusions will vary with each company, but they should stimulate the reader to want to learn more about the company that is for sale, starting with reading the rest of the offering memorandum.

The executive summary is the part of the offering memorandum that will be read by the largest number of people, so it should paint as enticing a picture as possible of the company that is for sale. In a large company, it is the part of the offering memorandum (along with the financial overview pages) most likely to get copied and forwarded to the firm's senior management for review.

If a reader does not have a positive feeling about the company after reviewing the executive summary, he is not likely to read the rest of the offering memorandum nor pursue any further interest in a possible purchase. Alternatively, a positive reaction should cause the reader to form a positive impression of the company (usually beyond any previous impression) so that he reads further and develops a stronger interest in the available company.

AN OVERVIEW OF THE INDUSTRY IN WHICH THE COMPANY COMPETES. Following the executive overview, the offering memorandum will usually have a description of the industry in which the company for sale participates. Generally, this section will be three to four pages in length, sufficient to give a reader a good overview of the general marketplace in which the selling company competes.

Included in this section should be a general overview of the industry (including historical and projected sales growth rates), key trends (including a list of items that are likely to enhance future industry growth), and a discussion of the competitive environment. In the section on competition, it is common to list the selling company's four to six major competitors (usually a short paragraph on each one), as well as to include a brief discussion of the strategies the selling company uses to compete successfully against its competitors. These may consist of such things as (1) a more competitive pricing structure (permitted because of cost efficiencies), (2) higher quality products or unique product characteristics, (3) better customer service, or (4) a superior reputation.

A DESCRIPTION OF THE COMPANY. This will be the longest section in the offering memorandum. Generally, it will cover the following information:

- **Corporate history**. This should include when the company was started and key milestones in its evolution.

- **Summary of product lines**. This should describe the key products or services that the company offers to each customer group. For example, in the food industry, a firm may offer product variations to various customer groups (such as supermarkets, club stores, and foodservice operators), and these differences should be described.

For packaged items, product packaging size may also vary among different end users (smaller sizes for supermarkets, larger sizes for club stores and foodservice customers). There should be a breakout of the percentage of sales to various end-user groups (e.g., 55 percent to supermarkets, 20 percent to club stores, and 25 percent to foodservice operators). Finally, where it is relevant, there should be a breakout of the percentage of products that are branded versus unbranded (or private label) items.

- **Sales and marketing procedures**. This section should describe how the company's products or services are marketed. For example, do they have their own sales personnel, or do they use third parties such as brokers? Do they call directly on retailers (including chains) or do they go through distributors? There should also be a general discussion of the marketing tools that the firm uses to promote sales of its products (such as consumer or trade advertising, direct mailing promotions, discount programs, and distributor promotions).

- **Discussion of distribution system**. Included in this section should be a summary of how products get from the production facility to the end user. Does the company have regional warehouses? Does it use its own trucks to deliver products to a customer's warehouse, does it rely on customers to pick up the items at the company's point of production or regional warehouse, or does it use third-party common carriers? If the selling company is a distributor itself, does it deliver to end-user customers? If the firm has several vehicles, these should be listed, including year and make.

- **Description of operations**. For firms that make products, this section should describe all aspects of the manufacturing process, from the time ingredients or other components enter the facility until they leave as finished products. The section should indicate at what percent of capacity the plant currently operates, and how much capacity could be expanded without capital expenditures (for example, by adding more weekday or weekend shifts). It is also appropriate to describe the procurement process used by the company.

- **Facilities**. This section should begin with a description of the company's facility(ies), including the age, capacity, and land controlled. It should also indicate whether there is room on the land for additional plant expansion and, if so, how much. This section should also indicate whether the facility is owned or leased and, if it is leased, the term and potential renewal options. Finally, the section should list the key equipment used by the company in the manufacturing process.

- **Personnel**. This section should indicate the total number of employees that the firm has, and how the number breaks out by type of employment (e.g., how many work in the plant, how many are in sales, how many work in finance or other office positions, and how many are senior managers or executives). There should be a brief biographical summary for each of the top four to six positions. This section should also describe the company's employee benefit programs—including vacation and sick leave policies, number of holidays observed, health/dental/life insurance offerings, and pension/IRA/401(k) retirement and savings plans.

- **Other items**. It is appropriate to include information on such other relevant items as patents, trademarks, and trade names owned by the company. Inclusion of information on the company's computer hardware and software would also be appropriate.

DISCUSSION OF FUTURE GROWTH POTENTIAL. After describing the company's current operations, the offering memorandum should next focus on the firm's future outlook. What is its growth potential, and what assumptions is that based on? Here it is appropriate to discuss the potential for introducing new products, entering new markets, and adding additional geographical territory.

The intent of this section is to try to paint an attractive picture of the company's future outlook. We are trying to show that the company is still in the "bud" stage, has not yet reached "full bloom," and still has lots of opportunity for future growth. The buyer of a company wants to buy it on the basis of its future outlook, not its past achievements. Thus, to optimize the value received for the company, the seller needs to convey the feeling that the firm has a bright future and that in fact its best days lie ahead. Obviously, if the outlook for the company is not particularly attractive, this section will need to be condensed but should still paint as good a picture as possible about the future outlook.

FINANCIAL INFORMATION. The section on financial information should provide a good summary of the company's financial history, its current financial status, and its projected financial outlook. My firm uses a single page to summarize five years of financial history and three years of projections (including the current year). Included for each year are sales, cost of goods sold, gross margin, selling and marketing expense, general and administrative expense, earnings before interest and taxes (EBIT), depreciation and amortization, and earnings before interest, taxes, depreciation, and goodwill amortization (EBITDA). We also include a one-page summary of balance sheet information for the past five years.

There should be a narrative discussion in the financial section that describes key aspects of each of the two financial schedules. For example, if cost of goods sold has varied much from year to year, we explain that. We try to put ourselves in the shoes of the reader by anticipating the questions he might have about the financial schedules and then answering them. A reader should have a good working understanding of the company's financial condition after reviewing this section. Sometimes copies of audited financial statements for the company are put in the appendix to provide additional insight on the selling firm's finances.

APPENDIX. Offering memorandums commonly contain an appendix. Included in it may be marketing brochures, promotional selling materials, sample advertisements, and favorable feature articles on the company. Pictures of the facility (both outside and inside) are also commonly included in an appendix. The purpose of these materials is to give the reader some additional positive, and usually colorful, information on the company, along with any particularly favorable press material. Other items that might be included in the appendix include an organization chart and a plant flow diagram, as well as audited financial statements.

How Much Detail Should Be Provided?

In deciding how long to make an offering memorandum, keep two things in mind. It should be long enough to tell the story of the company well. You want the readers to have sufficient detail so that they can form a well-founded opinion of the company and will be able to make an informed preliminary offer should they choose to. At the same time, you do not want to make it so long that readers get tired of wading through it or even get lost in the flow of the narrative.

I have often heard people say that an offering memorandum tends to repeat itself. To some degree that is by design. Frequently, key information will appear in the executive summary, be repeated in much greater detail in the company description section, and may show up again in the section discussing the company's future or its finances. It builds on the old adage that in a speech you should repeat yourself three times: at the outset you tell the audience what you are going to tell them, then you tell them in the main body of the speech what you want them to hear, and at the end you summarize what you have just told them. It is a key to getting the audience, or in this case the reader, to retain the important points made.

There is sometimes a tendency to put excessive financial information in an offering memorandum. Like an overly long and detailed narrative, this can bog down a reader and cause him to lose sight of the key message you are trying to convey. The summary financial tables I have described are critical to include. Likewise, charts can be useful for conveying key trend lines and stressing important directional information about a business.

I do not, however, think that you should put several pages of financial detail in the main body of an offering memorandum. If you want to go beyond baseline financial information, put it in the appendix. Better yet, leave it for the due diligence process, when only those who survive the first round of bidding will see it. There is no need to provide an enormous amount of confidential financial information to those who have not yet put forth an acceptable preliminary offer.

WHAT SHOULD BE EXCLUDED?

In addition to items that are overly detailed, will lead to excessive length, or get the reader lost in minutiae, there are other things that should be omitted from an offering memorandum. First and foremost is any information that could hurt your business if it were to fall into the hands of competitors. Even though each firm getting a copy of the offering memorandum will first be required to sign a confidentiality agreement, some employees of certain firms may not adhere to the strict terms of the agreement.

Thus, you should not include the names of customers or suppliers if it is proprietary knowledge. In most instances it would not be appropriate to include employee wage rates and salary information, or even detailed information on the terms of employee benefit programs. It is good to indicate that you provide health and dental insurance, for example, and that employees share in that cost. But you do not have to divulge the details of the program in the offering memorandum.

I would, in fact, take a conservative position in preparing an offering memorandum and leave out any information that a competitor could use against your business if he had it. Your financial results are not the most proprietary information you need to shield, in my opinion. Rather, it is information on your customers and employees.

WHO SHOULD DO WHAT IN PREPARING THE OFFERING MEMORANDUM?

If you decide to retain the services of an intermediary in selling your business, the intermediary should assume the overall responsibility for drafting the offering memorandum. He should be familiar with the key items to include and should be adept at writing such documents in a professional manner. The intermediary will usually prepare an outline of the offering memorandum and make sure the business owner is comfortable with the topics to be covered. He should also provide a list of information that he will need for the preparation of the offering memorandum. An owner should discuss the general availability of the information on the request list, indicating what may be readily available and which items will require special preparation time. An owner may want to appoint someone on his team to coordinate the information that is pulled together and to work directly with the intermediary to make sure that the requested information is in the form needed.

Once the intermediary completes a working draft of the offering memorandum, the owner should review it very carefully and should have appropriate people in his organization also review it. The information in the offering memorandum will be scrutinized by prospective buyers, and it needs to hold up under their due diligence examinations. It can be quite embarrassing and undermine credibility if information contained in the initial key document proves to be inaccurate. While a disclaimer at the outset of the document can reduce legal liability, lost credibility can be much more difficult to deal with. Thus, an owner should make sure that all the information is as correct as he can reasonably make it before the offering memorandum is completed.

CHAPTER SIX

BEGINNING THE SELLING PROCESS

PREPARING THE LIST OF PROSPECTS TO CONTACT

Once the offering memorandum is completed, the next step in the selling process is to begin contacting prospective buyers. This, of course, should be preceded by much thought on whom to contact. The owner of the business will have ideas about some good prospects, and if he engages an intermediary, that person or firm should be able to suggest numerous others to consider contacting. If the intermediary is knowledgeable about your industry, he will have thoughts about firms he knows or with which he has had contact.

An intermediary should also research the industry for the seller. Most industries have directories listing the key players in them. Some of these directories are published by industry associations, and many associations will sell their directories to interested parties. For example, when I did work for a client in the popcorn industry, I was able to purchase a good industry association directory listing the key firms in the popcorn business, their executives, and telephone numbers.

Many industries also have comprehensive directories published by independent firms. Chain Store Guide, for example, publishes comprehensive directories on a number of industries, including: foodservice distributors, supermarket chains, restaurant chains, drug store chains, home furnishings retailers, apparel stores, and many other industries. Each directory commonly lists firms by state and by product line. The lists usually have a brief description of each firm, which typically includes its sales, product lines, key personnel, and telephone and fax numbers. Thus, one can build a pretty complete list of industry participants who might be interested in a given company.

When an owner meets with his intermediary (if he selects one) to exchange the names of prospects on their respective lists, there should be considerable duplication between the two lists. As I noted earlier, if I have done my homework well, I should have 75 to 80 percent of the names on my prospect list that an owner has on his. I should also have numerous other names on my list that are not on the owner's list.

The owner and the intermediary should then consider each firm on the two lists and discuss the reasons that it would be appropriate to contact the firm. I like to discuss all the names on both lists, even those that are duplicates, because the owner's reasons for including a given company may provide me with additional insight about the company that will be useful when I contact the firm. The final list of prospects should be one with which both the company owner and the intermediary are comfortable.

WHO ARE THE BEST POTENTIAL BUYERS? An owner might develop a list of prospects based on firms that have contacted him in the past, saying "If you ever want to consider selling your business, please keep me in mind." In addition, an owner will likely know the names of other firms in his industry that have been growing by acquisition. The owner may also know of firms that would complement his company by product line, by having contiguous territory, or by having complementary customers. All of these should generally be on the list of prospects to contact.

Larger regional or national firms should be given particular consideration if the business fits well with theirs, because they usually are better able than smaller firms to pay cash or to issue publicly traded stock for acquisitions. Competitors should usually be given special consideration, as they are the most likely to have synergies that could result in higher cost savings, enabling them to offer more than other firms. Purchasing a competitor may also enable a buyer to compete more effectively in a given industry—providing it with more critical mass, as well as potentially giving it the opportunity to increase margins.

There is another large group of prospects that should be given serious consideration—financial buyers. These are firms that have pooled investments from a variety of individuals or organizations and who seek to acquire companies with the idea of growing them and then selling at a significant profit in three to five years. In the mid-1980s such firms were able to purchase companies by putting as little as 10 percent down in equity and borrowing the rest. In the years since, the amount of equity required for such purchases has increased steadily to about 45 to 50 percent.

With much less leverage, it has become more difficult for such firms to generate the returns that their clients earned on their investments 10 to 15 years ago, and thus some of them tend not to bid as aggressively as they did then. But, where they have acquired several firms in a given industry and can spread their cost base over additional volume to reduce unit costs, financial buyers can still be aggressive bidders.

Normally, financial buyers seek firms with a management team that will remain with the business and continue to run it for the three to five years they plan to own it. In return, most financial buyers will allow the management team to have a 10 to 20 percent ownership participation in the new structure, with the opportunity to share in the gain when the firm is sold a second time. This may not be attractive for an owner who wants to sell his business in order to retire or to pursue another endeavor, but if he has a well-trained organization under him with a leader who can step into his shoes, a sale to a financial buyer could still be worth pursuing, particularly among those financial buyers who already own firms in the same industry or who can bring other potential synergies to the seller's company.

And, for an owner willing to continue as a part of the management team for three to five years after the closing, a sale to a financial buyer can be attractive. He and his management team probably will be able to retain ownership of 10 to 20 percent of the company's stock. The financial buyer will provide the capital for growth (so the owner will not have more of his money at risk). At the same time, the owner will be able to take most of his money out of the business and diversify his holdings into other investments. And, the original owner will also get a "second bite at the apple," so to speak, when the company is re-sold three to five years later; presumably the second sale price will be significantly higher than the first due to the company's growth since the first sale, and the original owner should get a nice gain on his remaining investment in the company.

SHOULD ALL COMPETITORS BE CONTACTED? When I talk to clients about potential names to put on a prospect list, the biggest question is usually whether to contact direct competitors. Owners who have competed against a given firm for decades simply may not want to see their business became a satellite of that competitor.

Usually an even greater concern to an owner is that word of his interest in selling his company may get out to the competition's sales organization and it, in turn, might use such information against his company in the marketplace. Even if the business is sold within a short time, this can be disruptive—creating uncertainty among some customers, for example—but it will be of considerably greater concern if the business does not generate the kind of offers the owner wants and he decides to retain his company. Then, the owner has the bigger problem of calming down customers who were told by a competitor that this business was going to be sold and they should, therefore, shift their sales to a "more certain" supplier.

If an owner absolutely does not trust a competitor and feels that it would use knowledge of his interest in selling against him, then that competitor should not be contacted. But, where competitors, and particularly their leaders, are deemed honorable, I would encourage a seller to contact them. After all, a direct competitor potentially has the most to gain by buying your business. The competitor might be able to consolidate facilities (or at least make more productive use of each firm's plants by focusing on different items in different plants); it probably can reduce personnel (it will not need two separate financial or personnel departments, for example); and it should be able to cut other forms of overhead such as headquarters or regional offices. All of this would lead one to believe that direct competitors should be the best prospects for maximizing the selling price.

As we will discuss shortly, concern about word getting out into the marketplace can generally be controlled by going directly to the owner, CEO, president, or vice president of development of a potential buyer and requesting that they not share the information with anyone in their organization except on a need-to-know basis. I would also stress to them concern about word of any conversation getting out to their sales organization, who are the most likely people to use such information to try to take away your customers. When the importance of confidentiality is stressed to those at the highest level, if they are honorable individuals, the information will generally be confined to a small group.

HOW MANY FIRMS SHOULD BE ON THE CONTACT LIST? There is no magic number of companies that should be on a prospect list. For some businesses, there may be only 10 to 15 firms that an owner and his advisors feel are worth contacting. But I have found that doing a thorough job of canvassing prospects typically involves contacting 40 to 50 firms. Often the list will grow as the contacting process evolves, with additional prospects emerging through further thought and new insight.

My own rule of thumb is to call every firm that an owner and I feel might have both a serious interest and the financial resources to afford the purchase, except for firms whose confidentiality an owner does not trust. If in doubt, I lean toward calling, because you never know the thoughts going through a given CEO's mind about potential expansion. I cannot tell you the number of times I have called a prospect that I thought would have limited interest, but who, in fact, became a serious bidder. At the same time, you do not want to contact a firm unless you feel there is a potential fit, because when making each call you want to be able to explain why you thought the firm might have an interest in your business.

CONTACTING POTENTIAL BUYERS

WHAT PERSON IN THE ORGANIZATION SHOULD BE CONTACTED? Before the contact process begins, the list of prospective companies should include the address, telephone number, and fax number for each firm, as well as the name of the contact person and his position. Such names are commonly available in industry or association directories. Where you have only the name and phone number of a company, you can call the number and usually get the rest of the information you need from the company receptionist or phone operator—including the street address and P.O. box number, fax number, and the name of the person who holds the position you are seeking to contact (e.g., owner, CEO, president).

In selecting the person in each company to contact, I usually try to talk to the highest-placed person in the organization that I can—the owner, the CEO, or the president. The top person is the key decision-maker with the ultimate authority to decide whether to pursue a given acquisition and to determine how much to bid for a company he is interested in. Thus, why not try to talk to him directly and tell him about the available business? That way your message will not be filtered through an assistant or lower-level person.

There are, of course, situations in which I do not seek out the top person in a prospective buyer's organization. The larger the company, the more difficult it will be to make an initial contact with the CEO. Thus, if I learn from talking to the CEO's personal assistant, for example, that the chief financial officer or the vice president of corporate development handles all acquisition work, I will call him instead. This person is still high in the organization (generally reporting directly to the CEO), usually knows whether the firm would have a potential interest in the available company, and usually is experienced in handling an acquisition, including getting a confidentiality agreement signed.

WHAT SHOULD BE SAID DURING THE FIRST CONTACT AND THE INITIAL FOLLOW-UP? I believe that the first contact with a prospective firm should be by phone rather than by mail. Too often letters get screened out by an assistant before they get to the intended recipient. Or, a letter may end up in a large pile of mail that receives only a quick glance when the recipient returns from an extended trip. Because there are so many ways for letters to get misdirected, lost, or ignored, I prefer to use phone calls followed by faxes (faxes are usually given a higher priority than mail by administrative assistants).

Once I reach the person I am trying to call, I briefly introduce myself and my firm, and then indicate that I have been retained by a client whose business I thought might be of interest as a possible acquisition. I then briefly summarize some key facts about my client's company—what products it has, its general size in sales (I do not reveal profits), and recent growth rates (if significant). Next comes the key part: summarizing why I think my client's company would be a good acquisition candidate for the firm I am calling. I will then ask if the person I'm talking to feels his company would like to consider the business I represent as an acquisition candidate.

If he says he is interested, I tell him I will be happy to provide him with a copy of the confidentiality agreement and that, when he has signed and returned it, I will send him a copy of the offering memorandum. Once he agrees to sign the confidentiality agreement, I tell him the name of the company, since he will see who the company is when he receives the confidentiality agreement. I then fax the confidentiality agreement to him, and when I receive a return fax of it that has been signed, I send him a copy of the offering memorandum, usually by overnight mail.

On the other hand, if after listening to my initial description of the company, the person I have contacted is unsure about his level of interest or requests more information on the company, I will offer to fax a two-page overview of the business. This information piece does not disclose the name of the company, but it will have more information about the company and what it does. It will also usually list key investment considerations— reasons why a firm should give serious consideration to the company as an acquisition prospect. These will generally include, in shorter and more generic form, the same key investment considerations listed in the offering memorandum, items such as:

- Strong historical and projected growth.

- Potential to greatly expand sales through new products being developed.

- A high percentage of branded products or services.

- A market share leader.

- Attractive production facilities with significant expansion potential.

- A strong management team willing to remain with the business.

About three days after I fax the overview to my contact, I follow up by phone to make sure he received it, as well as to ascertain whether he would like to sign a confidentiality agreement so he can receive the offering memorandum.

Frequently, the person you are seeking to contact will not be available when you call him. In such cases, I usually leave a short voice-mail message in which I explain why I was calling, state that I am faxing a two-page company overview that will provide more information on the acquisition prospect, and leave my telephone number with a request that he call me at his convenience. I then write a cover letter to accompany the faxed company overview.

In the cover letter I indicate that I am following up on my voice-mail message, explain why I think the available business would be a good fit for his company, outline the procedure for signing a confidentiality agreement to receive a copy of the offering memorandum, and again invite him to call me at his convenience. Here, too, I follow up about three days after sending the fax to make sure he received the information I sent and to try to find out if he is sufficiently interested to sign a confidentiality agreement so he can see the offering memorandum.

If the person is not available the second time that I call, I usually try to work with his secretary or personal assistant to verify receipt of the material that I have previously faxed. In many cases the assistant will recall receiving the material; if not, I will generally re-fax the cover letter and two-page company overview. Then, I will ask how we can best work together to get a response to the material from the CEO or president. Usually, the assistant will promise to talk with the boss and make sure he has reviewed the material and then either get back to me with his reaction or else have him call me directly.

Sometimes it takes repeated follow-ups to get a definitive response about a firm's level of interest in the business; be persistent, but always be friendly. Sometimes the CEO is traveling, on vacation, or otherwise unavailable for several days. But, by working with his administrative assistant, you will usually ultimately get a call from him, or receive word through the assistant about his level of interest.

How Do You Maintain Confidentiality in the Marketplace?
Maintaining confidentiality starts with how you and/or your intermediary handle the first contact with each prospect. First, talk only to a key decision-maker in the company—the owner, CEO, president, or other executive who is responsible for acquisitions. Then, as I mentioned earlier, tell that person your concern about the confidential nature of the subject that you are going to discuss. Do not divulge the name of the business unless the key decision-maker to whom you are talking agrees to sign the confidentiality agreement. Conclude the initial call with a reminder of the importance you attach to confidentiality, making sure that he keeps it within a small group of decision-makers and, particularly in the case of competitors, stress concern about word leaking out to the marketplace through his sales organization.

While there is no guarantee that word will not leak out into the marketplace, I have found that talking directly to responsible persons and stressing the importance of confidentiality to my client usually has prevented any information leaks. Once the preliminary bids are in and an owner has received indications that the price proposals are in line with his expectations, the prospect for a sale increases and the need for confidentiality is no longer as crucial.

If, however, the initial bids are less than what an owner had set as his minimum and he decides not to pursue a sale any further at the present time, then it is important to keep as confidential as possible the fact that an exploratory selling effort was undertaken. All confidential offering memorandums should be recalled, and the firms that received them should again be reminded of the importance of adhering to the confidentiality agreement.

There are times when, despite all reasonable efforts to maintain confidentiality, word of the selling process leaks out. In such cases, it is important to try to identify the source of the leak and to go directly to that source with your concern. On one occasion I was seeking to sell an agribusiness operation. All efforts at maintaining confidentiality seemed to be working. But one day the owner called me and stated that his organization was hearing in the marketplace that a certain firm was letting out word about the selling effort.

Upon learning this, I called the owner of the business that had allegedly released the information. I did not accuse him of an outright violation of the confidentiality agreement, but I told him what we had heard in the marketplace, reminded him strongly of the terms of the confidentiality agreement he had signed, and said that we took that agreement very seriously. I further stated that, if we heard any further rumors that were attributable to his firm, we would request an immediate return of the offering memorandum and would have to weigh the possibility of legal action. To the best of my knowledge, my conversation put a stop to further leaks from his organization.

FOLLOWING UP AFTER THE INITIAL CONTACT

THE CONFIDENTIALITY AGREEMENT. If the response to the initial contact is positive and the prospect has stated a willingness to sign a confidentiality agreement in order to receive a copy of the offering memorandum, the next step is to send out a copy of the confidentiality agreement. I usually fax it to the owner or corporate executive to whom I have been talking. I try to keep the content of the confidentiality agreement short (holding it to one page if possible), but it needs to cover the following key elements:

- **A description of the information to be kept confidential.** This will usually include any information supplied to the prospective buyer (both orally and in writing and both initially and at any other time during the selling process).

- **Information that will be excluded.** This usually includes information that (1) was known to the potential buyer prior to the time the confidentiality agreement is signed, (2) becomes known during the term of the agreement through other sources not covered by the confidentiality agreement, or (3) is in the public domain.

- **Term of the agreement.** I usually suggest a three-year term, and almost always get it, because that is long enough to be effective for the seller and short enough for a potential buyer to accept.

- **Who will have access to the confidential information.** This will usually be limited to employees of the potential buyer who need to know because of their involvement in the evaluation process, as well as the firm's bankers, public accountants, and attorneys.

- **Return of the information.** The agreement should provide that, once a firm is no longer evaluating the company as a prospective acquisition, it will return any confidential documents that were provided (or certify in a letter that they have been destroyed). The firm should also certify that any copies or notes developed in conjunction with the analysis have been destroyed.

Some attorneys may want to add provisions to spell out in greater detail potential violations of confidentiality if the two firms are direct competitors. They may also seek to add other provisions, such as specifying (1) the state whose laws will govern any litigation surrounding deemed infractions of the confidentiality agreement and (2) the jurisdiction where claims must be filed. I do not feel that the latter two are an absolute necessity, since the selling company will usually be the party to file a claim if there is one to be filed, and it can select the location (usually where it is based) where it wishes the case to be adjudicated.

Once a prospective buyer has signed and returned the confidentiality agreement, it should be countersigned by the selling company, which should then send a copy back to the prospective buyer. That way each company will have a fully executed copy of the agreement.

Finally, make sure that you have professional help in drafting the confidentiality agreement or in reviewing one supplied by a potential buyer seeking to make a preemptive bid. One of my clients had been talking to another firm about purchasing his company. Shortly after retaining us to represent him, my new client received a confidentiality agreement from the firm that was considering making a preemptive bid for the company. The form was an agreement that obligated **both** firms to confidentiality. I pointed out to my client that it was not fair to ask him to sign an agreement which bound him as well as the other firm, because he was not interested in purchasing the other firm and thus would not be receiving confidential information on it. I gave him an alternative form that only obligated the other firm, which the interested party then signed.

SENDING THE OFFERING MEMORANDUM. Once the confidentiality agreement has been signed, the offering memorandum should be sent. I usually do this by overnight mail for several reasons. First, I feel that timely delivery is more certain (I can track it and make sure it got to the intended recipient). Second, it lands on the desk of the owner or senior executive of the prospective buyer in a more important fashion than regular mail; it may, in fact, be hand-delivered by his assistant and either given to the recipient directly or placed in the center of his desk for immediate attention upon his return. Third, it conveys a greater sense of urgency to the prospective buyer. I give a higher priority to items sent by overnight mail when they arrive on my desk, and I think most other executives do as well.

A day or two after the offering memorandum was scheduled to arrive, I usually call the owner or senior executive to verify that he received it. I also use this as an opportunity to see if he has any initial questions and also to inquire about their evaluation process. I want to know how extensive their evaluation process is likely to be and to verify that they will be able to comply with the timetable we have established for getting preliminary valuations of the selling company.

ANSWERING QUESTIONS. Once the offering memorandum has been reviewed by the owner or senior management of the prospective bidder, that firm will usually have questions. You should establish clearly at the outset of the selling process who will be the point person to handle all contacts with, and questions from, other firms. This is so you will not have prospective buyers with questions calling various individuals in your company, disrupting operations and perhaps getting different responses. If you have retained an intermediary, he should be the conduit for channeling all questions to the selling firm. The intermediary, in turn, should firmly tell all potential bidders that under no circumstances will direct contacts with the selling company be tolerated and that any such violations will result in a firm being dropped from the evaluation process.

If you do not retain the services of an intermediary—or other professional to coordinate the selling process—you need to appoint one person on your senior staff to handle such inquiries, as it is usually best if the owner stays above the ongoing questioning process. Just as when an intermediary is used, the prospective bidders need to understand that this senior executive is the only one in the company to be contacted.

The person serving as the communications link with prospective buyers should be in touch with each prospective buyer periodically between the time the offering memorandum is received and the preliminary bids are due (usually within four to six weeks after receipt of the offering memorandum). His role is to make sure each prospect gets its questions answered sufficiently to enable it to submit a meaningful preliminary bid.

This does not mean that you should provide highly sensitive information, such as more detailed financial statements than in the offering memorandum, customer names, or detailed information on employees. These items can be supplied at a later date to the finalists—both to conserve the amount of work that has to be done for a variety of companies and, more important, to preserve sensitive information until finalists go through the initial due diligence phase. In addition, such information will usually not materially affect the preliminary valuation a firm submits.

Bidders should raise any questions they have with the person handling the communications between the selling company and prospective buyers, and that person should be able to answer most questions directly. If he cannot, the intermediary—or other designated contact person—should talk to the appropriate person in the selling company, get the requested information, and convey it to whoever asked the question.

Occasionally, it will be appropriate for the person handling the communications with prospective bidders to get an executive of the selling company on the phone with a prospect to discuss an item that is very important to the prospect. Even in these cases, the person handling communications (e.g., the intermediary) should also be a party to the conversation. That way he can jump in if the questioner raises issues that should not be addressed at this stage in the process; also the intermediary (or other contact person) will know exactly what information was given to the inquiring firm, which can be important if that person later claims he was told something different.

WHAT ADDITIONAL INFORMATION SHOULD BE MADE AVAILABLE, AND WHEN? As you can see from the discussion above, I am not one who believes in supplying a lot of information—beyond that contained in the offering memorandum—to prospective buyers during the preliminary bidding process. Keep in mind that a well-prepared offering memorandum will have extensive information on the company or business for sale—certainly enough for most firms to determine whether they have sufficient interest to submit a preliminary valuation or a general range within which that valuation would fall. The preliminary valuation is non-binding and can always be made subject to verifying certain assumptions and getting additional information during the due diligence phase.

Some firms will indicate an interest in buying a firm and will sign the confidentiality agreement, but their real goal is to get more information on a current competitor (or a potential competitor if they are considering entering the industry sector). If the seller tries to answer all their requests for additional information, he could end up giving out information they may use against the selling firm in the future, the confidentiality agreement notwithstanding. Clearly, this could hurt the owner if he ultimately decides not to sell and continues to compete against them.

Even if the owner ends up selling the company to another party, the buyer could find itself with several competitors who have enough sensitive information about its newly-acquired business to create an unfair competitive situation. For example, if one were to share sales or pricing data about key customers to an unsuccessful bidder, that firm might use the information to take away volume that it would not otherwise have been able to obtain.

After preliminary bids have been received, a seller should be willing to supply some additional information to the few firms selected to go into the next stage. During this phase of preliminary due diligence, additional items supplied might include: copies of leases, a more detailed list of equipment, a list of employees (without names) and their compensation by department, Phase I environmental audits (if available), an aging of accounts receivable (without listing company names), and audited financial statements.

After final bids have been received and a designated buyer has been selected, it will be appropriate to release additional information in the final phase of due diligence. This might include copies of tax returns (particularly if the stock of the company is being sold), detailed financial records for the past five years, and the names of key customers (along with the volume each does).

At each stage, a potential buyer is being required to provide a more certain commitment before it may proceed to the next stage of getting more detailed and more sensitive information on the selling company. The most sensitive information should not be released until a formal agreement has been reached between the buyer and seller and there is little risk that the transaction will not be completed, thereby limiting the chance that the information will be held by someone who is not the ultimate buyer of the company.

CHAPTER SEVEN

SEEKING OFFERS FOR THE BUSINESS

GETTING PRELIMINARY BIDS AND PURCHASE PROPOSALS

SENDING OUT THE LETTER REQUESTING PRELIMINARY BIDS. After prospective bidders have had the offering memorandum for three to four weeks, it is customary to send a letter requesting a preliminary valuation from each of them. The letter should include an update of any significant information about the company that has changed since the offering memorandum was prepared. This might include a more recent balance sheet, especially if the fiscal year has ended since the offering memorandum was printed or if the most recent balance sheet shows a significant change in working capital items. In such cases, one usually requests that interested parties use the most recent balance sheet in preparing their preliminary bids.

In addition to a more recent balance sheet, it is important to provide an updated profit and loss statement, particularly if it shows that recent sales and earnings are in line with or exceed the projections made in the offering memorandum. Finally, if the company has secured any major new customers or has experienced other key developments, it is appropriate to include information on them in the letter requesting preliminary bids or as an attachment to the letter.

The letter requesting preliminary bids should include the following other information:

- The date that the preliminary bids are due (this will typically be two to three weeks after the letter is sent).

- The person to whom the preliminary bids are to be sent (usually the person coordinating the selling process, such as an intermediary), including the address and phone and fax numbers.

- A statement as to (1) whether bids may be made only for the stock of the company or (2) whether a prospective bidder may express its valuation in the form of either a stock or an asset purchase.

- A request for a list of any additional information that the bidder would like to receive about the selling company and any due diligence that it would expect to conduct before making a final offer.

- A reiteration of whom to call with any questions about the information in the offering memorandum or about the selling process in general.

CLARIFYING WHETHER BIDS MAY BE FOR EITHER STOCK OR ASSETS. As noted above, it is important that the letter requesting bids clearly states whether the seller will only accept offers for the stock of the company or will accept bids for either the stock or the assets of the company. While the **net** valuation between a stock or an asset purchase may be comparable, the **gross** valuation may be significantly different between the two forms of purchase, depending on whether any interest-bearing debt will be assumed under an asset purchase.

Typically, in an asset purchase in which the buyer assumes only such non-interest-bearing liabilities as payables and accrued expenses, the valuation will be higher by the amount of the interest-bearing debt not assumed. But the extra amount is then used at closing by the sellers to pay off the debt. This will net out the same amount to the shareholders that a stock purchase would have where the debt was assumed directly by the buyers.

A bidder may also be willing to bid more for an asset purchase in order to have the opportunity to write up the assets and take more depreciation to reduce taxes. When the stock of a company is purchased, the buyer typically has to use the values of assets on the books of the company being purchased and cannot write up their values, so there is less depreciation to deduct for taxes. There can be exceptions to this, as when a transaction is done using a 1044(h)(10) election, named after the corresponding section in the Internal Revenue Code. Under a 1044(h)(10) election, the form of the transaction is a sale of stock, but the buyer is permitted to account for the transaction as if it were an asset purchase, and therefore is able to write up the assets and take increased depreciation.

Valuations may also differ between a stock and asset purchase if there are any potentially sizable off-balance-sheet liabilities, such as litigation or a possible environmental clean-up. If the seller does not indemnify the buyer for potential damages from such liabilities, the buyer will want to discount the effective price paid for the transaction under a stock purchase (where the buyer assumes the liabilities of the company) compared to a purchase of assets (where the off-balance-sheet liabilities of the company generally are not transferred to the buyer).

An additional factor that may result in different valuations for selling the stock of a company versus a sale of its assets would be a potential tax difference to the sellers. If there is a potential large tax recapture that the sellers would have to pay in an asset sale but which would not exist in a stock sale, the effect of this on the overall value will have to be evaluated by both parties. Sometimes a buyer and a seller will agree on a somewhat lower effective price for the stock of the company than a buyer would be willing to pay for the assets of the company, and both may come out ahead. The buyer pays less initially, and the seller avoids any tax recapture that would reduce his after tax proceeds (I will discuss more about tax recapture a little later).

RESPONDING TO PRELIMINARY BIDS. Two or three days before the preliminary bids are due, it is appropriate for the person coordinating the selling process to call each of the firms that received an offering memorandum. During these phone conversations, he should make sure that each prospect is aware of the due date, clarify what is expected in the "bid letter," learn how they expect to send the bid letter (e.g., by fax or overnight mail), and answer any questions. On the afternoon of the date the bids are due, it is appropriate to call once again any bidders who have not been heard from and make sure they are still planning to submit a bid letter.

Once the preliminary bids have been received, the intermediary may have to call some of the bidders to clarify information in their letters. The intermediary needs to put all of the bids on a common basis so he can help the seller understand the differences between the bids and the net impact that each bid would have.

Depending on how many bids are received, it is usually desirable to select four to five firms for the next round, which will consist of preliminary due diligence. You want enough firms to ensure that you will have competing final bids from at least two to three firms, but you do not want to take firms through the due diligence process if their preliminary bid is well below the most attractive proposals or below what a seller would be willing to accept.

It is often worth going back to lower bidders to indicate how much they would have to raise their preliminary bid in order to be invited into the next round. Often firms will raise their preliminary bid in order to get into the next round. One should, however, try to verify that such a bidder is still serious at a higher valuation level, so that the bidder and the selling company do not needlessly waste their time going through even the preliminary due diligence phase.

In addition to asking lower bidders to raise their preliminary bids, sometimes it is also appropriate to let some of the higher bidders know that they will need to raise their valuations if they are going to ultimately be successful in purchasing the selling company. I have often advised firms that they can go into the next round only if they raise their bid to a certain level to be within range of other key bidders. I have also told runners-up that they bid high enough to get into the next round but they were not among the best bidders. That lets them know that they probably will have to increase their final bid to become the ultimate winner.

OVERSEEING PRELIMINARY DUE DILIGENCE

Once the bidders for the next phase have been selected, the selling process turns to preliminary due diligence. Usually each company selected for the next round will be invited to spend up to a day at the office of the company being sold. Several days prior to the visit, the person coordinating the selling process should get a list of each prospect's information requests so that as many of these can be accommodated as practical.

If you engage an intermediary, he should work with the selling company to help prepare its executives for the due diligence meetings. This should include preparing a list of the written information that will be made available to prospective buyers to review during their visit. It should also include helping the senior executives of the selling company prepare the presentations they will give during the company visits. Such preparation should start several weeks ahead of time—even before the preliminary bids are received—so that there will be sufficient time to prepare, edit, and practice the presentations prior to the first bidder's visit.

The morning of each bidder's visit typically starts with the intermediary (or person who is coordinating the selling process) welcoming the visitors and outlining the agenda for the day. The owner, president, or general manager of the business usually follows with an overview of the business, its recent history, its projected growth over the next three years, and a description of the company's management team. This is followed by the leader of each key discipline summarizing important aspects of his area.

The chief financial officer generally will talk about the firm's financial condition and provide more details about the numbers in the offering memorandum. The head of sales and marketing (sometimes two individuals) will discuss his operations— describing the firm's products or services, its customer base, sales strategy, selling organization, and marketing tools. The head of human relations will cover information about the firm's employees, compensation plans, and benefit plans. The production or operations executive will cover the key aspects of his discipline. Depending on their importance to the selling company, such other areas as information systems (talking about the firm's computer capabilities) may also be covered.

The presentations usually wrap up with the intermediary reviewing the key investment considerations that prospects should consider in making their final bid. Typically, he will cover many of the same reasons that were included in the executive summary of the offering memorandum, detailing why the firm would make an attractive acquisition. After each of these presentations, there should be adequate time for questions from the visiting company. Typically these discussions will consume most of the morning, and are followed by a catered box lunch.

Shortly before, during, or after lunch, it is appropriate to let the representatives from the visiting firm meet with their counterparts from the selling firm—the finance people can go into more detail on their discipline, the sales and marketing people can do the same, and others can pair off likewise. This provides a good opportunity for the visiting company to gather much more information on the prospective acquisition than if all questions were posed to the whole group.

The final activity of the day is usually the opportunity to visit a data room. Here, there are copies of important documents such as major contracts, lease agreements, and detailed financial information that prospective bidders will want to review before making final bids. The following is a typical list of items that may be found in the data room.

FINANCIAL INFORMATION

1. Copies of audited financial statements for the past three to five years

2. Copies of financial statements for the months since the last year ended, along with results for the same periods for the previous year

3. Copies of five years of tax returns (may also be withheld until a later date)

4. Copies (or summaries) of all insurance policies

HUMAN RESOURCES

1. Copies of the employee handbook (if one exists)

2. Copies of employee benefit plans

- Health and dental insurance plans
- Retirement plan
- 401(k) plan
- Profit sharing plan

- Stock option plan (including a list of positions covered)
- Any other benefit plans

3. Lists of employees by job position (with compensation but not names)

MARKETING

1. Copies of promotional sheets highlighting new items and specials

2. List of products sold

3. List of the top 10 customers by sales dollars and percent of total sales (no names)

4. List of the top 10 suppliers by dollars purchased and percent of total purchases

OPERATIONS

1. List of all major fixed assets in production facilities

2. List of vehicles by type, size, age, and make

LEGAL

1. Copies of facility lease agreements

2. Copies of truck lease agreements

3. Copies of major contracts

Even though each prospective buyer who is invited for a visit will have signed a formal confidentiality agreement, a selling company should not feel it needs to provide copies of all items in the data room for prospective buyers to take with them. Those items the selling company is comfortable releasing may be made available by having a copy for the prospect to take back to its offices (e.g., a copy of the employee handbook, which summarizes key benefit programs). A prospect may request a copy of certain other information in the data room, and the selling company may want to hold that request for a while; it can send copies later of those requested items which it feels can be shared without harm.

Sometimes a prospective buyer will have certain information requests beyond what was covered during the visit. These should be given to the intermediary or person coordinating the selling process, so that he can discuss them with the selling company before responding.

GETTING FINAL BIDS AND
FORMAL PURCHASE PROPOSALS

A couple of weeks after the due diligence meetings have been completed, the person coordinating the selling process should send out a letter requesting final bids. The letter should go out about two to three weeks before the bids are due in order to permit each bidder to wrap up its evaluation process and gain necessary approvals prior to submission of a bid.

The letter requesting final bids should include some of the same items as in the letter requesting preliminary bids, as well as certain other items. This letter typically will include the following:

- The date that final bids are due.

- The person to whom the final bids may to be sent (usually the person, such as the intermediary, who is coordinating the selling process), including the address and phone and fax numbers.

- A statement as to (1) whether bids may be made only for the stock of the company or (2) whether a prospective bidder may express its valuation in the form of either a stock or an asset purchase.

- A list of any contingencies to which the bid may be subject, such as:

  - Approvals (board and/or shareholder approval).

  - Financing (what steps, if any, are necessary to get financing in place to cover the purchase price, and how long that will take).

  - A list of any remaining due diligence that the bidder needs to conduct prior to signing a formal purchase agreement.

- The bidder's plans for the selling company's management and whether it intends to close any facilities in the near term.

- The length of time that the bidder expects to need before being able to close on the transaction.

- A reiteration of whom to call with any questions about the process.

Sometimes an intermediary will enclose a draft definitive sale agreement with the bid request letter, and will ask each bidder to mark any changes it wants in the draft. The marked-up draft of the definitive sale agreement is then to be sent back with the final bid. This enables the selling company to understand the extent of the changes the prospective buyer wishes to make.

It clearly puts pressure on a bidder to agree to items favoring a seller (such as weaker seller's representations, a shorter indemnification period, and a lower cap on the dollar amount of indemnification). This also greatly reduces the time for negotiating a formal definitive sale agreement, and it circumvents the customary practice of the buying firm drafting the definitive sale agreement. And, it also significantly reduces uncertainty about the items that the buyer might request later if normal negotiations were held on the definitive sale agreement.

All of these things work to the advantage of the selling company when a marked-up draft of the definitive sale agreement must accompany the final bid. If a firm offers the highest bid but makes changes to the draft of the definitive sale agreement that the selling company does not like, the intermediary can go back to the bidding firm and indicate that the offer will be accepted if the bidder eliminates certain of the changes it is requesting in the definitive sale agreement.

Once the final bids are received, the intermediary may need to call certain bidders to clarify items in a proposal. Just as with preliminary bids, the intermediary needs to be able to articulate to the seller the net value of each proposal, so that a decision can be reached on which one to accept.

Even if a bid is in an acceptable range, a seller may still request that the intermediary tell the highest bidder that it will get the nod if it raises its bid by a specific amount. Usually, a bidder will be willing to raise its offer a little if it knows that in so doing it will definitely be the winner. Likewise, if there are two firms whose bids are close to one another, it is appropriate to go back to each and try to get them to enhance their proposals in a kind of run-off event.

KNOWING WHEN TO ACCEPT A GOOD OFFER

Any owner who sells his business always wants to feel that he got the best possible selling price. I just discussed potential ways to go back to bidders and seek further price enhancements, and such tactics are usually worth pursuing. But, sometimes an owner will overplay his hand, so to speak, and try to hold out for an unrealistic price. A good intermediary should educate an owner early in the selling process on what price is reasonable to expect; in most cases this usually helps an owner develop a realistic price expectation. Despite such coaching, however, sometimes an owner's expectations will accelerate as the selling process proceeds.

I recently had a client whose business had about $15 million in sales annually. While the company had a good history of growth, recent sales had slipped and the outlook for the year deteriorated as we proceeded through the selling process. We got preliminary bids from five firms—all of them financial buyers rather than strategic players in the industry. Four of the five bids were right in line with what I felt the business was worth. The fifth bid was about 30 percent higher than the others. It was all cash and had several other attractive features.

I thought we had a "home run offer," one the owner would jump at. Instead, after considerable reflection, he made a counter-offer that was about 15 percent higher than the best offer. The highest bidder—turned off by the owner's lack of appreciation for its very attractive bid—refused to raise its offer. I did my best as an intermediary to try to explain to the owner the attractiveness of the offer he had received, but he did not want to move. When the owner refused to drop his counter-proposal, the bidder lost interest and the sale was not consummated.

It is still difficult for me to fully appreciate why this deal did not get completed. Perhaps the owner changed his mind about really wanting to sell as he began to realize the profound impact a sale would have on his life. I also think that the owner was greatly disappointed that no major industry player appreciated his business enough to make an attractive bid (his company was really too small to have much impact on large strategic players), and the owner, for whatever reason, did not want to sell to a financial buyer.

In any case, the owner turned down a higher price than he will be likely to get for a long time. He missed a golden selling opportunity. The last time I checked, his sales and earnings had slipped further, and he could no longer tout his company as a growth vehicle, as we had been able to do during the marketing process.

My point here is that an owner can demand too much. He can become unrealistic in his expectations—or lust to sell to a strategic buyer rather than a financial buyer—to the point where it causes him to turn down a very attractive offer. Now, this owner will probably have to work several years past his targeted retirement age, and his retirement, when it comes, will be shorter and probably less comfortable financially than it could have been. An owner wants to get as much as he can for his business, but should not get stubborn and overplay his hand.

Another factor to weigh in assessing when to accept an offer is knowing when a bird in hand is worth two in the bush. A few years ago, I represented a firm whose sales and earnings had slipped significantly after several years of growth. This is never the best circumstance in which to sell a business, but as the seller's representative, I put together a marketing document with the most positive story that I could. I received a couple of serious offers; both were from industry players who recognized that the company still had some good competitive positions despite slipping sales. The best and most serious bidder also realized that unless it was able to purchase the firm soon, sales were likely to deteriorate to the point where there would no longer be sufficient critical mass to justify a purchase.

The majority owner of the business that was for sale wanted to hold out for a higher price than any of the more than 50 firms I had contacted felt was warranted. Thus, no sale took place. When a sale finally did occur a couple of years later, the price was a fraction of what had been offered two years earlier. The owner had let the solid offer (the bird in hand) get away in hopes of someday finding a higher offer (the elusive two birds in the bush). When the business continued to deteriorate, the two birds in the bush never materialized and the bird in hand had long since flown away. The moral of the story is that, if a business is starting to slip and the owner has no solid evidence it will quickly turn around, he is usually well advised to take the offer in hand rather than hoping for something better down the road.

What to Do If You do not Receive
an Acceptable Offer

While I believe the marketplace generally tells an owner what the appropriate value is for his business, there are times when a worthy buyer does not emerge or the best price offer is really lower than the owner and his advisors all feel is appropriate. Obviously, the intermediary can go back to the firms making the most attractive proposals and try to work out a mutually acceptable price.

If the bidder, however, will not raise his offer, or at least the amount paid at closing, there may still be ways to structure the sale that will benefit the seller. Perhaps, for example, the buyer can be persuaded to add an earn-out so the seller will get a second payment in a few years based on the selling company's performance after the closing. Or, perhaps the buyer purchases a majority of the stock of the company at a given price, and then has an option to purchase the rest using a formula based on future earnings, which will likely result in a higher price for the seller when the minority portion of the stock is sold later. Or, perhaps the seller can negotiate a higher price based on providing some seller financing—with the buyer paying for part of the transaction through a three-to-five year loan from the seller.

But sometimes no buyer emerges, at least initially, who is willing to pay a price acceptable to the owner. In such an event, the owner will probably need to retain control of his business for the near term, while seeking to improve its financial performance, with the expectation of going back to some of the previously interested parties—and perhaps new ones—once the outlook improves.

The key thing to remember if you do not receive a reasonable bid initially is not to give up. It took me over four years to successfully extract one of my clients from a slowly dying business. We had to overcome what at times seemed like insurmountable obstacles. Many times my client felt he would not survive financially during the extended process, but neither of us ever gave up. In the end we convinced a developer to build a 16-story cooperative apartment complex on the land his small business had previously occupied. In the process, we liquidated his business and sold the land separately. By selling them separately, my client received much more than his business and land on which it sat had ever been worth when linked together. It took longer than either my client or I had hoped, but we eventually turned a sow's ear into a silk purse.

There is another potential option that may be worth an owner's consideration if he does not receive a reasonable offer in the marketplace and if he does not wish to continue at the helm until prospects improve. That is an ESOP—an employee stock ownership plan. In essence, under an ESOP the employees purchase shares of stock from the owner, using the company's future earnings to provide the cash to buy the stock in annual installments. Initially, the employees usually purchase only a minority position in the company, and then each year purchase an additional percentage based on the cash flow of the company. Numerous business owners have successfully used ESOPs to transfer ownership of their companies to their employees while, in turn, receiving annuities for several years from the employees' ongoing purchase of the owners' shares.

CHAPTER Eight

DECIDING
WHICH OFFER
TO ACCEPT

Once the final bids and formal proposals are in and all points in them are clearly understood, the next step is to decide which offer to accept. This assessment process should begin with the intermediary developing a summary chart comparing all the key elements in each proposal. Obviously, price usually goes to the top among key determinants, but the probability of completing the transaction should also have a high priority in a seller's mind.

If the highest bidder has made its offer subject to certain contingencies, such as obtaining financing, the contingencies need to be weighed carefully. The last thing a seller wants to do is spend considerable time completing due diligence with a potential buyer, only to have that buyer fail to close because it did not obtain its financing or get other necessary approvals to complete the transaction.

It is difficult to go back to other bidders and try to re-ignite interest in the selling company several weeks after they have been told that the selling company decided to accept another firm's offer. Some bidders will have moved on to consider other expansion opportunities. Others may view the target company with some suspicion after the initial winning bidder has retreated to the sidelines.

Even if the reason for this can be easily explained, once the "winner" drops out, it is still likely to give runner-up bidders leverage to discuss a price that is lower than the original winner offered, and perhaps even lower than the runners-up offered. So, when a bidder is designated as the "winner" of the auction process, the seller wants to feel pretty certain that he will be able to close the transaction on the terms proposed.

There are several other factors that a seller should consider in determining which bidder to focus on and to negotiate with. Several of these are covered in the sections that follow.

ASSESSING WHETHER TO SELL STOCK OR ASSETS

Selling the stock of the company versus selling the assets of a company can have significant tax, as well as legal, ramifications. If the company is organized as a "C" corporation, it pays federal and state income taxes on its profits directly. On the other hand, firms that are organized as "subchapter S" corporations do not pay income taxes directly (but they cannot have over 75 share-holders). Instead, the company's income (or loss) is passed on to the owners in proportion to the percentage of ownership each has. This income (or loss) is then included in each owner's personal income tax return. Although it is not mandated, subchapter S corporations often make a cash distribution (if funds are available) to help each owner cover his tax obligation on the company's income.

When the stock of a company is sold—regardless of whether the selling company is organized as a C corporation or an S corpo-ration—no capital gains or other income tax is normally due at the corporate level. The owners of the corporation will individ-ually be responsible for paying capital gains taxes on the difference between the selling price they receive for their shares and the cost (or purchase) basis they have in their stock. Federal capital gains tax rates are about one-half of federal income tax rates, so a seller will normally want to have as much of the proceeds as possible treated as a capital gain rather than as ordinary income (more on this later).

Tax considerations get more complicated when a company sells its assets rather than its stock. If the selling company is organized as a C corporation, it will be liable for paying capital gains at the corporate level on the sale of the assets. The selling company may also have an additional income tax liability if it has taken accelerated depreciation on any of the assets that are being sold (which is tax recapture).

Moreover, individual shareholders will also be liable for paying capital gains tax on any gain they personally receive from the sale. This occurs when the company selling the assets is subsequently dissolved and the cash that remains from the sale (after corporate taxes are paid) is distributed to the shareholders. Each shareholder then has a capital gains tax obligation based on the difference between the proceeds he receives and the price he paid for his shares in the company.

The tax consequences of selling assets—rather than stock (where a corporation has no capital gains liability)—become more complex if a company has changed its organization from a C corporation to an S corporation during the ten years immediately preceding the sale. In that case, the corporation has a capital gains liability on the difference between the value of the company ten years ago and its value on the date on which it changed to an S corporation. There would be no capital gains obligation for the corporation between the time the company became an S corporation and the sale date.

Let's assume, for example, that the owner switched from a C corporation to an S corporation five years prior to the sale. Let's further assume that the owner can establish that the company's value ten years ago was $12.5 million. (This can generally be arrived at by an independent appraiser taking the earnings for the year immediately preceding the start of the ten-year period and multiplying it by a P/E multiple that would have been common at that time for businesses of comparable size, growth rate, and industry position.) Let's also assume that five years later when the owner decided to convert to an S corporation, he had his company appraised and its value had risen to $23.5 million.

Even though the sale price might now be $60 million, there is no capital gains tax liability at the corporate level for the difference between the $60 million selling price and the $23.5 million value when the company shifted to an S corporation. There is, however, a corporate capital gains liability for $11 million—the gain in the company's value between the start of the ten-year period preceding the sale ($12.5 million) and the company's value immediately before it changed to an S corporation ($23.5 million).

The bottom line of this discussion is that a seller will usually prefer to sell the stock of his company, especially when it is organized as a C corporation. If the owner of a C corporation sells assets, he will incur double taxation (taxes at both the corporate and individual levels). Selling assets has far fewer adverse tax consequences if the selling company is organized as an S corporation, especially if it has been one for ten years.

Besides tax considerations, there are legal reasons for which an owner will usually prefer to sell the stock of his business rather than just its assets. When a buyer purchases the stock of a company, it usually also assumes the legal liabilities of that entity. Thus, any uncollected debts, environmental liabilities, unpaid tax liabilities, or unfunded pension liabilities or other employee claims would be the ultimate responsibility of the buyer of the selling company's stock. Such potential liabilities can be substantially reduced or "collared" through an indemnification in the definitive sale contract that states that the sellers of the company will reimburse the buyer for various obligations that the buyer may incur from specified liabilities.

Obviously, a buyer's perspective on whether to purchase the stock or the assets of a selling company differ from a seller's perspective. Whereas a seller usually prefers to sell stock—especially if his business is organized as a C corporation—a buyer usually prefers to buy assets. An asset purchase automatically reduces a buyer's legal liabilities; even with a well-written indemnification from the seller, some legal risks usually remain with a stock purchase.

An asset purchase also gives a buyer an opportunity to write up the value of the acquired assets to market value from the depreciated value carried on the selling company's financial statement; this conserves the buyer's future cash flow by permitting more depreciation (and thus more of the purchase price) to be written off for tax purposes. As noted earlier, when the stock of a company is purchased, the buyer usually has to use the values on the books of the company being purchased and cannot write up their values, so there is less depreciation to deduct for taxes.

So how do a buyer and seller reconcile their different preferences for a stock-based or an asset-based transaction? Sometimes, it comes down to a negotiated price. If it is very important to a seller that stock rather than assets be sold—perhaps to avoid high double taxation because the selling company is organized as a C corporation or to avoid a major tax recapture problem (caused by having taken accelerated depreciation)—the seller may find it worthwhile to take a lower price than he might command for an asset sale. At other times, where there is limited potential to benefit from being able to write up the assets, a buyer may agree to accept the purchase of stock, but then insist that the seller indemnify the buyer so that the legal liabilities are effectively not much greater than they would be in an asset sale.

Some years ago, I represented a buyer who was involved in an acquisition and really wanted to purchase assets rather than stock, primarily to minimize any legal liabilities it might otherwise inherit. The seller was equally adamant about wanting to sell stock, largely because an asset transaction would trigger a major tax recapture problem (caused by accelerated depreciation and other write-offs) that would cost it millions of dollars. In fact, if the buyer would not purchase the stock of the entity rather than its assets, the seller was ready to turn to another bidder who was prepared to do a stock transaction.

We finally worked out a solution whereby the seller got a stock rather than an asset transaction, but the buyer got the seller to pledge specific hard assets (with a combined value equal to about one-half the purchase price) behind the seller's indemnity, thereby greatly enhancing the buyer's ability to collect against the indemnity should the need arise.

The reason the buyer insisted on hard assets as security behind the seller's indemnity was because the selling company had recently been acquired by a financial buyer who could have put the assets of the seller into a new subsidiary that would not have been responsible for claims by the buyer. By essentially carving out specific assets to stand behind the indemnity, the security would remain intact during the indemnification period. This compromise allowed both parties to receive the item most important to each. The seller got a stock sale that saved it millions of dollars in tax recapture, and the buyer got substantial security behind the seller's indemnification.

In other instances, the buyer may prefer to purchase assets primarily so it can write up asset values, while the seller prefers to sell stock to avoid a tax recapture. As noted in Chapter Seven, the issue may sometimes be resolved by structuring the transaction using a 1044(h)(10) election under which the form of the transaction is a sale of stock, but which permits the buyer to account for the transaction as if it were an asset purchase, and therefore write up the assets and take increased depreciation. This, coupled with the seller's strong guarantee or indemnification for potential liabilities, could provide a "win-win" for both companies.

WEIGHING WHETHER TO KEEP PART OF THE COMPANY

While most owners sell their entire company (either in the form of stock or assets) at one time, there are instances when it might be advantageous—or even necessary—for an owner to retain a portion of the company's stock for a period of time. This may be particularly true if a financial buyer is deemed to be the best overall bidder.

As noted earlier, financial buyers are investors who purchase firms with the idea of re-selling them at a higher price in three to five years, as opposed to strategic buyers who own and operate other businesses in the same industry and plan to retain a purchased company indefinitely. Financial buyers usually prefer that a business owner remain with the business after a sale, and that he and his management team retain between 10 and 20 percent of the company's stock in order to provide a significant financial incentive to achieve (and hopefully surpass) sales and earnings goals established prior to the closing. Being part of the ownership going forward—and thereby having the opportunity to benefit in a substantial manner from a higher price when the company is re-sold by the financial investors— keeps the management focused on maximizing growth of the company's bottom line.

If an owner is willing to stay on in a leadership role after the sale, this structure can be beneficial. It gives the owner cash for selling a high percentage of his ownership, thus enabling him to diversify his investments and do appropriate estate planning. But, by retaining a minority portion of the company, he is able to have a second bite at the apple, so to speak. If the earnings grow as planned, the company probably will be worth more in a few years, and the original owner will be able to share in that higher price with the minority position that he retained.

While purchasing less than 100 percent of the stock is usually done by financial buyers, it also is done occasionally by strategic buyers. Many years ago when I worked for General Mills, it decided to go into the restaurant business and agreed to purchase the small chain of Red Lobster seafood restaurants. General Mills originally purchased 95 percent of the stock of the company from Bill Darden, Red Lobster's founder.

At the time, Bill had only four Red Lobster restaurants, but he had solidified a concept that General Mills felt could be rolled out across the country. General Mills provided the capital and Bill Darden provided the leadership to open hundreds of Red Lobster units throughout the country. A few years after purchasing the original 95 percent of Red Lobster, General Mills bought the remaining 5 percent—and paid substantially more for that 5 percent than it had paid for its first 95 percent. It proved to be a good selling structure for both Bill Darden and General Mills.

In deciding whether to sell all of a company initially or to retain a minority position for a few more years, the owner must first decide whether he wants to remain active in the business. If he does not, it is probably best to sell his entire ownership up front. If the owner is willing to remain active in the business, retaining a minority portion in the company can be advantageous. But before an owner agrees to follow that path, he should make sure the following are true:

- He should have a good management team who will remain in place to help run the company.

- He should believe that the company will appreciate in value over the next several years, enabling him to receive a significantly higher price per share at that time than it currently commands.

- He should feel he will be able to work closely and comfortably with the new owners and will have appropriate autonomy to run the business.

If an owner decides to pursue such a structure, he would also be well advised to have an acceptable exit plan in place at the time he sells majority control to the new owners, so he can leave the company should serious differences emerge down the road. This plan should include a formula for selling the remaining shares at a price based on how well the company has done since the original sale.

One other aspect to keep in mind is that, when less than 100 percent of the company is sold, the transaction has to be for stock rather than for assets. As discussed in the preceding section, a stock sale compared to an asset sale can be quite advantageous to the seller, especially if the business is structured as a C corporation. Selling 90 percent of the stock of the company could result in more after-tax proceeds for the owner than selling 100 percent of the assets, especially if the latter sale were to trigger capital gains taxation or a major depreciation recapture at the corporate level. What the owner ultimately receives for the remaining 10 percent of the stock could be viewed as a bonus above what a 100-percent sale of assets probably would have brought.

DECIDING ON THE FORM OF PAYMENT

Another consideration that an owner needs to weigh in deciding which buyer to go with is how the purchase price will be paid. There are advantages to taking all cash, but there can also be benefits to receiving all or part of the purchase price in stock. And, sometimes it can be advantageous to both the buyer and the seller to structure the sale with a somewhat lower payment at closing followed in a few years by a performance payment based on the subsequent results of the company. The following sections review each of these options and their various pluses and minuses.

TAKE ALL CASH AT CLOSING. When a seller takes the entire purchase price in cash at closing, he eliminates any uncertainty about potential future payments, as well as the future value of any stock that he might take in lieu of cash. The old adage that "cash is king" sums up why many feel it is the preferred form of payment. With cash, a seller can immediately reinvest all the proceeds any way he wants. But, whenever cash is taken in a sale, it is subject to capital gains tax for the year in which it is received.

TAKE STOCK OF THE BUYER. Taking stock in the buying company in return for stock in a seller's company can have two key potential advantages to a seller. First, if stock is taken in a solid, publicly traded firm, it may have attractive appreciation potential. If the stock of the acquiring firm is valued at $30 per share at the closing and it doubles to $60 in five years, the seller has doubled the value of the proceeds he received for his company. Moreover, that share appreciation is on a pre-capital-gains-tax basis, which allows greater overall appreciation than a seller would achieve if he were to take cash, pay the associated capital gains tax, and then buy shares in the acquiring company.

The second advantage of taking stock instead of cash is capital gains tax deferral, where such taxes are deferred until an individual sells the shares of stock received in the purchase of his business. (Note: You cannot defer capital gains by taking stock unless the sale is structured as a sale of stock rather than as a sale of assets.) If the seller takes "registered stock" (defined below) in a publicly traded firm, he can sell his stock in blocks of shares whenever he wishes—he does not have to sell all the shares received at once. And, capital gains tax is due only on that portion of the stock sold. If 10 percent of the stock received is sold in a given year, capital gains taxes are due only on that portion, not on the 90 percent retained.

A seller should keep a couple of things in mind if he is considering taking stock in the company buying his firm in exchange for the stock of his company. Make sure that the stock in the acquiring company is highly liquid. This involves making sure the shares received are "registered" securities, meaning they can be sold by the holder anytime he wishes. The alternative is "lettered stock," which would require the holder to go through the expensive process of getting the shares "registered" before he could sell them publicly. "Registered stock" has been registered by the company under security regulations, and registered shares that are not held by shareholders are generally held by the company as "treasury shares." Treasury shares can be readily issued for acquisitions.

Lettered stock, not having been registered by the company under security regulations, can only be traded privately, thereby greatly limiting its appeal. To get lettered stock registered can be a very expensive and time-consuming process. Thus, the value of a specific number of shares of lettered stock may differ greatly from the value of the same number of shares of registered stock. To minimize this problem, a seller might require that the issuing company register the shares received by a certain time at the buying company's expense, so that the seller can sell the shares he receives on the open market whenever he desires.

Liquidity is also enhanced when the shares issued by a company are publicly traded and have significant daily trading volume. If there is substantial daily trading in a company's stock, it greatly facilitates a seller's ability to dispose of a large amount of stock in a relatively short time without unduly depressing its price per share. On the other hand, if the issuing company is relatively small and/or has a relatively low number of its shares traded each day, and the seller has a sizeable block of shares that he wishes to dispose of, it may take an extended period of time to complete the selling process in an orderly manner. This is because putting a major block of shares of a thinly traded stock on the market at one time could significantly depress the value received for the shares.

If liquidity is a problem with the buyer's stock, a seller may want to have an agreement that will require the buyer to repurchase part or all of the shares used for the transaction within a given time frame. Normally, under such an arrangement, the price paid by the company repurchasing its shares will be either the market's closing price for the shares on the day of the repurchase, or the average trading price during that day.

A seller may request the buyer to stipulate that the price paid per share on the repurchase date will be no less than its trading price on the original closing date, so that the seller does not have a downside risk in taking part or all of his proceeds in stock. If the buyer will not agree to this, perhaps it will agree to a minimum stock price somewhat below the price at closing, which would still reduce the seller's potential downside risk.

Finally, when considering taking stock, make sure that you have faith in the future of the buyer's company. While postponing capital gains is good conceptually, it is of no value if the price of the stock of the buying company falls during the years after the closing.

While future stock prices are always uncertain, it is worth weighing the historical trends of the stock you will be receiving against the stock market as a whole, and particularly against similar companies in the same industry. If its performance has been sub-par, and if there is nothing on the horizon to cause one to believe that its future performance is likely to be better than it has been historically, then you may want to avoid taking stock and insist on cash instead. In such instances, cash may be preferable even if it would result in a somewhat lower price than if stock were taken.

TAKE A COMBINATION OF CASH AND STOCK. Since both cash and stock have their respective advantages, it may be worth considering taking a combination of the two. Usually, if at least one-half of the purchase price is taken in stock, that portion taken in stock has capital gains taxes deferred until the new stock is sold. Of course, the portion that is taken in cash is immediately subject to capital gains taxes.

Taking one-half in stock and one-half in cash, for example, would give a seller greater liquidity than he would have had before a sale and the potential to do considerable estate planning. But, taking one-half in stock would defer 50 percent of the capital gains and provide the opportunity for stock appreciation with pre-tax dollars. Of course, the potential concerns discussed above about taking all of the proceeds in stock would also be true if some portion of the selling price is taken in stock, although the risks would be reduced by taking at least part of the selling price upfront in cash.

Using a combination of cash and stock can also be advantageous to the buying company—particularly if (1) it is publicly traded, (2) the acquisition is relatively large, and (3) it wishes to keep its ratios of debt and equity within a certain range. Using all cash will likely force the buying company to take on more debt, which in turn may leverage up its balance sheet to a higher ratio of debt to total capital (long-term debt plus equity) than it would prefer (or than its bond rating agency would accept without lowering its debt rating). Alternatively, using all stock for a relatively large acquisition may lower the buying company's earnings per share (EPS) more than it would find acceptable (the more shares divided into the earnings of the company, the lower the earnings per share will be, after taking into account the earnings the acquired company will add).

Thus, in making a large acquisition, a company may wish to use part debt and part stock to keep its balance sheet ratios in line, while also minimizing EPS dilution. Even when individual acquisitions are relatively small and no single transaction would have a significant adverse impact on balance sheet ratios or cause meaningful EPS dilution, an acquiring company still needs to keep such issues in mind as it executes an acquisition program. Thus, when not using a combination of stock and cash for a specific acquisition, buying companies often pay cash for some of their purchases and then equalize the impact on their balance sheets by using stock for other acquisitions.

HAVE A PERFORMANCE CONTINGENCY. In many sales, the seller believes that his business is worth more than potential buyers do, often because of different views on how fast future profits will grow. A performance contingency is frequently used to bridge such differences. Under this structure, the buyer and seller agree on a base price, usually close to what the buyer feels the company is worth. The buyer then pays that amount at the closing. But, the buyer also agrees to pay the seller an additional amount if sales and/or profits reach or exceed certain pre-determined target levels in the future, often three years. This gives the seller the potential to realize the extra price that he may feel his company is worth beyond what a buyer is willing to pay upfront. This sort of performance contingency is commonly referred to as an "earn-out."

There are a couple of things to keep in mind when deciding whether to structure a sale with a performance contingency. First, unless the seller remains in the position of running the company during the earn-out period, he will no longer have direct involvement over how the company is operated or how the books are kept. For example, the buyer could merge the acquired company with the rest of his operations, making records for the acquired company difficult to maintain and rendering the allocation of income and expenses highly subjective.

In addition, even if the acquiring company is able to keep accurate records for the selling company, it may decide to depress the acquired company's profits during the earn-out period by investment spending to accelerate the acquired company's growth. This would reduce the potential amount the buyer would owe the seller during the earn-out period but enhance the earnings that might accrue to the buyer in later years.

For these reasons, sometimes a seller will prefer to base any contingency payment on sales of the acquired company's product lines, perhaps on the number of units sold rather than their dollar value. It is usually easier and less arbitrary to track sales rather than profits. Thus a buyer does not have an incentive to depress sales the way it might depress profits by investment spending for growth in future years at the expense of near-term profits. The part of the selling agreement that deals with the contingency payment needs to be very carefully drafted. The seller and his attorney need to try to anticipate any issues or concerns that might arise in how performance is managed and computed. This is important so that the seller has as much certainty as possible of receiving a fair payment for the performance his company experiences during the earn-out period.

One of the companies for which I worked purchased a business that enabled it to diversify into a new area. Since it was a new area, there was uncertainty about making the financial projections that the sellers felt could be achieved, even though the sellers were quite confident that the projections were reasonable. The two firms agreed to a purchase price to be paid in cash at closing. In addition, they agreed on a three-year earn-out period, with an additional amount to be paid based on the earnings achieved during that period. The sellers agreed to remain with the business and continue in their same managerial roles, as did the rest of the sellers' management team.

During the three-year earn-out period, the acquiring firm made several other acquisitions to expand its base in this new area, putting each new acquisition under the management of the originally purchased company. The buyer and the sellers of the originally purchased business had agreed upfront on a formula that the originally acquired company would use to pay the buyer for the financing it supplied to make additional acquisitions. Each acquisition subsequently made was identified and recommended by the owners of the company originally sold. During the earn-out period, the sellers of the original company met their earnings target each year, and at the end of the three years, the buyer paid the sellers the maximum payout specified in the original purchase agreement. It proved to be a winning transaction structure for both the sellers and the buyer.

DECIDING WHETHER TO USE A LETTER OF INTENT

Once a seller has decided on the potential buyer it wishes to deal with and has reached agreement on the basic terms for a transaction, the two parties next need to decide whether they want to commit the basic terms to a memorandum of understanding. The alternative generally would be to go directly from oral agreement to development of a definitive sale agreement. If a written memorandum of understanding is used, it is generally referred to as a "letter of intent." Generally, letters of intent are not legally binding contracts (unless certain parts of them provide otherwise); they simply outline the basic terms on which the two parties have reached agreement. A letter of intent can be useful in setting forth the basic parameters of the planned transaction and providing a framework for the more detailed negotiations that will follow during the preparation of the definitive sale agreement.

While a letter of intent in total is usually not legally binding, a buyer may request that it contain a binding provision that the seller negotiate solely with the designated buyer for a specified period of time, such as three to four months. The rationale for the buyer to request such a "standstill period" is that it wants to have sufficient time to complete its due diligence and negotiate a definitive sale agreement without worrying whether the seller will continue to have discussions with one or more other parties. The buyer will commonly argue that it is going to invest a significant amount of time and money in conducting due diligence and incurring legal fees and that these should be offset by having a window of exclusivity.

Before a seller agrees to such a window of exclusivity (or standstill period), he should be far enough along in the negotiations to conclude there is a high probability that the transaction will be completed successfully. In addition, a seller may want to insist that any window of exclusivity have (1) checkpoints whereby certain items have to be completed or agreed to by certain dates and (2) a provision to keep the terms of the definitive sale agreement in line with those in the letter of intent.

Deviation from either of these items (without approval by the seller) would give the seller the right to talk to other parties. Such a provision will generally keep the buyer on schedule to complete its due diligence, and it should keep the negotiations within the framework of the original agreement. As a result, it tends to level the playing field between the buyer and seller when the seller agrees to give a window of exclusivity.

Letters of intent provide a moral commitment from both parties to proceed in good faith to develop the definitive sale agreement. In this regard, they can provide a useful backdrop for more comprehensive discussions that will follow. But, by the same token, letters of intent are not an absolute requirement. Parties acting in good faith can move directly from developing an informal understanding of basic terms to the definitive sale agreement.

NEGOTIATING THE DEFINITIVE SALE AGREEMENT

Once a seller has decided which offer to accept and has agreed on the basic terms—including price, form of the transaction (a sale of stock or assets), and form of payment (cash, stock, or a combination)—he and the buyer will shift their attention to negotiating a definitive sale agreement. This is the binding contract that will cover all the specific terms and conditions surrounding the sale. Since a definitive sale agreement has broad implications for a seller—both in terms of potential major financial liabilities and the length of time such commitments survive the closing—this chapter is longer and more comprehensive than others in this book. It is extremely important for a seller to understand the implications of the primary components of a definitive sale agreement.

The team negotiating the definitive sale agreement commonly consists of one or two attorneys for the seller and one or two attorneys for the buyer. In addition, the buyer and seller will usually each have one or two business representatives in these sessions. If intermediaries are used by either party, they may also be included. From time to time, specialists in certain functional areas (such as human resources or taxation) may be invited to join the discussions. Sessions are typically held in the conference room of one of the attorneys.

Generally, it is considered the buyer's prerogative to prepare the first draft of the definitive sale agreement, although there may be exceptions. For example, in an auction process, a seller often will submit a draft contract for bidders to mark up and return with their final offers. In such instances that marked-up document will then form the basis for subsequent discussions on the agreement and, depending on the comments the buyer's attorney made at the time the final bid was submitted, there may be no need for extensive further negotiations. But if the seller has not previously submitted a contract draft for the buyer's attorney to mark up, the buyer's attorney will usually submit the first draft of the contract.

SCOPE OF ITEMS USUALLY COVERED

The scope of a definitive sale agreement is usually quite broad. Obviously, key items such as purchase price, what is being sold (stock or assets), and the form of payment (stock, cash, promissory notes, or a combination) will be covered. In addition, the document should cover a number of other items. Generally, these will include such things as:

- A list of the definitions and key terms used in the contract.
- A description of the assets to be purchased and the liabilities to be assumed (in the case of an asset sale).
- A section governing the closing.
- A provision for an adjustment in the purchase price between the signing of the contract and the closing.
- Representations and warranties made by both the seller and the buyer.

- Indemnification by the seller.

- Provision for post-closing adjustments to the purchase price.

- The governing law under which any litigation will be adjudicated, and the jurisdiction for filing claims (e.g., if the representations and warranties are claimed to have been breached).

The sections that follow discuss each of these in more detail.

DEFINITIONS AND KEY TERMS

Early in the definitive sale agreement, it is common to have a section defining key terms used in the contract. Items commonly defined include such things as:

- Closing balance sheet

- Disclosure schedules

- Effective time of closing

- Employee benefit plans

- Encumbrances

- Environmental laws

- Financial statements

- Intellectual property

- Pre-closing period

- Purchaser

- Seller(s)

- Stockholders' equity

- Taxes

- Third-party claims

One may reasonably ask why is it so important to define such terms. Let's take taxes as an example. There are a wide variety of taxes, and both the buyer and the seller need to be clear on who has the responsibility to pay which taxes and for which time periods. The definitions section merely sets forth the full list of taxes and governmental assessments to be dealt with in the definitive sale agreement. The section will specify the jurisdictions to be covered (federal, state, local, foreign) and the type of taxes and assessments to be included (such as income, property, sales, excise, franchise, employment). Later, the agreement will specify whether it is the responsibility of the buyer or the seller to pay each tax or assessment and the time period for which each has responsibility for the respective tax or assessment.

A Description of Assets to Be Purchased and Liabilities to Be Assumed

In the case of an asset sale, the contract will have a section that describes the assets that are being purchased, as well as the liabilities that will be assumed by the buyer. For example, the description of the assets will identify the real estate that is included (the company may own other real estate that is not included in the sale, such as an owner's vacation home). This section will also provide whether the cash of the business is going to be transferred in the sale or retained by the seller (it often is retained by the seller).

Accounts receivable over 60 or 90 days may be excluded from the sale because the buyer prefers not to purchase receivables with a low probability of collection. The seller may also want to exclude old accounts receivable because if he includes them and guarantees their collectability, he may have to wait 60 or 90 days until the buyer turns them back to the seller; during this time it is unlikely that the buyer will spend much effort trying to collect them, since he knows he will get 100 percent of the amount from the seller whether he spends time trying to collect them or not.

On the liability side, the seller may retain the interest-bearing debt, for example, and pay that off with proceeds from the sale. Otherwise, the purchase price will likely be reduced dollar-for-dollar by the amount of interest-bearing debt the buyer assumes. Likewise, the buyer may not assume certain lease obligations, such as vehicles used by the owner; the owner may simply want to retain these leases. This section of the definitive sale agreement for an asset purchase spells out which items are being sold or assumed by the buyer and which the seller is retaining. Under a stock sale, the buyer usually gets all assets and assumes all the financial liabilities (although things such as the collectability of accounts receivable may still have to be guaranteed).

THE CLOSING

The section on the closing will state the date for the closing, as well as the exact time and location where the closing will take place. For example, the section may specify that the closing will take place on July 1 at 10:00 A.M. at the office of the seller's attorney. Because the closing may take several hours to complete, and it cannot be determined in advance exactly when it will conclude, the contract usually provides a specific time at which the closing will be effective. Often this will be at 12:01 A.M. on the date of closing. This means that the buyer will get the proceeds from any business done on the closing date and, likewise, will be responsible for any liabilities incurred on that date.

The definitive sale agreement should also stipulate under what circumstances the parties may agree to postpone the closing date. For example, the buyer may need additional time to get the transfer of a lease agreement approved, or the seller may need extra time to rectify a defect in the title of a parcel of property being transferred. Usually, the definitive sale agreement will permit relatively short extensions for such events (such as ten days). But, it also is common for both parties to agree on a "drop-dead" date on which the transaction will be either automatically terminated or may be cancelled by either party if it has not been completed.

If the transaction dies because the drop-dead date is reached for reasons beyond either party's control, there is usually no liability to either party for failure to close. But, damages could be assessed if one party proves that the other party deliberately tried to delay the transaction until the drop-dead date in an effort to avoid a closing because of a change in its desire to complete the transaction (or otherwise willfully breached its obligations under the definitive sale agreement).

ADJUSTMENTS TO THE PURCHASE PRICE BETWEEN THE SIGNING AND THE CLOSING

A buyer and seller will usually agree on a basic purchase price as one of the first items in structuring a transaction, but a definitive sale agreement involving a privately owned (versus public) company will usually provide certain conditions under which the purchase price might be altered between the signing of the agreement and the closing. There may also be post-closing adjustments to the purchase price, which will be discussed later, but the following describes adjustments to the purchase price that may be made prior to the closing.

ADJUSTMENTS DUE TO CHANGES IN BALANCE SHEET VALUES.

Typically, the purchase price will be pegged to the balance sheet prepared as of a specific date. For example, a purchase price of $35.5 million may be based on a December 31 balance sheet, with a provision that the purchase price will be adjusted upward or downward between December 31 and the closing date, which we will say is July 1. Between December 31 and July 1, the values on the balance sheet will probably change. The amount of inventory and receivables may be up or down and the liabilities—such as payables, accrued liabilities, and debt—may also have increased or decreased.

If the sale is for stock, the price is usually pegged to a certain level of goodwill (the amount paid above net worth), and the purchase price is adjusted upward or downward as of the closing date for any change in the value of shareholders equity. (If a business were sold for less than shareholder value—and thus had negative goodwill—the amount below shareholder equity would remain constant while the purchase price was adjusted upward or downward for any change in shareholders equity.)

Similarly, if the sale is for assets, the purchase price is commonly adjusted for the increase or decrease in the value of the assets to be acquired between the December 31 balance sheet and the closing date balance sheet. Likewise, the purchase price would also be adjusted for any change in the amount of any liabilities to be assumed. In both a stock sale and an asset sale, the amount of goodwill paid based on the December 31 balance sheet remains the same on the closing date. The change in purchase price merely reflects changes between the book values shown on the balance sheets on the two different dates.

Why is the purchase price adjusted for increases or decreases in the value of assets and liabilities between the original balance sheet and the closing balance sheet? If the closing date balance sheet has more assets on it than the December 31 balance sheet on which the purchase price was based, the buyer would be getting more assets for the same purchase price, and the seller would be giving the buyer more while receiving the same price. Likewise, if assets decline, say because receivables are lower, the buyer should not have to pay the same price, because the seller has already received a portion of the purchase price by collecting the amount that receivables declined between December 31 and the closing date. The same is true for any upward or downward adjustment in the value of assumed liabilities.

When a sale of stock is used, changing the purchase price for the difference in shareholders equity accomplishes the same thing. The change in shareholders equity nets out differences in both assets and assumed liabilities between the two balance sheet dates. Purchase price adjustments for changes in net worth between the two balance sheets, therefore, are made so that changes in the value of assets and liabilities are netted out to provide both the buyer and the seller with the same effective purchase price.

ADJUSTMENTS DUE TO CHANGES IN BUSINESS RESULTS. Sometimes the sale agreement will provide for an adjustment to the purchase price if business sales or profits undergo a meaningful change between the time the selling agreement is signed and the closing date. I once represented a buyer who wanted a downward purchase price adjustment if sales did not maintain a certain level between the signing and the closing.

The business was experiencing a decline in sales due to an economic slowdown, and the buyer was concerned that if sales dropped much further it would reduce the critical mass of the business being sold to an inefficient level, thereby significantly reducing profitability. The seller understood this rationale and agreed to a formula for adjusting the price downward if sales fell below a specified level. In addition, the buyer was given the right to cancel the definitive sale agreement and walk away from the transaction if sales fell below a second threshold level.

ADJUSTMENTS AS A RESULT OF DUE DILIGENCE FINDINGS. Most due diligence is customarily done before the contract is signed, and any adjustment to price that stems from due diligence is made prior to the signing. However, most definitive sale contracts permit a buyer to continue its due diligence between the contract signing and the closing.

As previously noted, the definitive sale agreement may provide for a price adjustment if there is a material change in the condition of the business between the signing and the closing. Even though the agreement does **not** contain such a provision, if the buyer discovers a material inconsistency in what the seller had previously represented and affirmed in the agreement, the buyer typically will not be obligated to close the transaction or may require the seller to agree to a lower selling price—even after the contract is signed—as a condition of completing the deal.

A few years ago, I had a client who had done extensive due diligence on a firm it wished to buy. After we thought we had a good understanding of the company, we agreed upon a price. However, we continued to go deeper into the company's records, and found that its outlook was not nearly as bright as had been represented to us. I successfully used this new information to negotiate a major reduction in the purchase price. The seller really had no option but to agree with the lower price we offered, because it was unlikely that he could go back to other bidders for the business and get a better price after he disclosed this new information.

REPRESENTATIONS AND WARRANTIES

I believe that second only to the stated price paid for a business, a seller should give his most serious consideration to the representations, warranties, and indemnification he makes in the definitive sale agreement. Representations and warranties are discussed in this section while indemnification is discussed in the next.

Representations and warranties generally serve two purposes. First, they provide a basis on which a buyer can come back to the seller and claim monetary damages for breach of contract if the representations or warranties are determined to have been inaccurate at the time they were either made or updated. Second, the accuracy of the seller's representations and warranties at both signing and closing is typically a condition of the buyer's accepting an obligation to consummate the transaction. Thus, representations and warranties provide a basis for the buyer to walk away from the deal in the event they are determined to have been inaccurate when the definitive sale agreement was signed **or** if they become materially inaccurate by the time the transaction is scheduled to close. It is, therefore, very important that a seller understand the representations and warranties that he is making and the potential impact on him if a breach occurs.

ITEMS USUALLY INCLUDED. While contracts differ in the scope of the representations and warranties made, the following items are usually covered as part of the sellers' representations.

- **Organization and authority of the corporation and its owners.** This attests that (1) the corporation is duly organized and in good standing under the laws of the state in which it is incorporated; (2) the corporation has authority to enter into the transaction (in the case of a sale of assets) and to operate the business as presently conducted; (3) the corporation has "X" number of shares of stock outstanding, all of which have been properly issued and are owned by the sellers (in the case of a sale of stock); (4) copies of the corporation's charter and bylaws have been provided to the buyer and are in full force and effect; (5) the owners have full authority to sell the stock or the assets being sold without the consent of any governmental authority or other third party and without violating any organizational document, contract, law, or court order; and (6) the owners have duly authorized the transaction.

- **Financial statements.** This attests that the historical financial statements for the past "X" number of years—as well as the interim financial statements for the current year—accurately and fairly present, in all material respects, the financial condition and operating results of the company as of the respective dates of the statements.

- **Environmental matters.** The increasing concern in recent years about protecting the environment, along with the possibility of incurring liability resulting from mere ownership of contaminated property, have resulted in a growing emphasis on assessing environmental issues and estimating potential environmental liabilities when buying a business.

  Buyers generally insist that, at a minimum, a Phase I environmental site assessment be prepared for each facility owned or operated by the seller. A Phase I assessment includes a general investigation of the history of the property being acquired, a search of public databases related to reported releases of hazardous substances, and an inspection of the property to look for evidence of spills or releases of hazardous substances.

  If a Phase I report indicates that hazardous substances were released on the property, then a Phase II assessment is usually conducted. A Phase II assessment generally includes an analysis of soil and/or groundwater samples taken from the property through test borings to determine the extent of soil contamination. In some instances, contaminated soil may have to be removed by the seller and replaced with clean dirt prior to a closing, or the purchase price may be adjusted to cover the cost of such soil replacement by the buyer after the closing.

  In any case, a buyer will typically look to the seller to make a representation that, aside from any contamination noted on an attached schedule, the seller is not aware of any other release of hazardous substances on the property. In addition, the seller will usually be asked to represent that the business has complied with all environmental laws and regulations, including laws related to the disposal of any hazardous substances.

Environmental representations can be the most potentially expensive representations a seller makes because, if it is discovered after the closing that the seller failed to disclose unlawful disposal practices employed by the seller's business, the seller could be saddled with an extraordinarily high cost to clean up the soil or groundwater.

- **Employee matters.** Another important area of representations deals with employee items. Here the seller will usually be asked to represent that all employee benefit plans (including pension plans, 401(k) matching programs, and profit-sharing plans) are fully funded as of the closing date and that there are no undisclosed employee liabilities.

  It is also common to request a representation that no employee benefit programs have been operated in violation of any governmental requirements. (In another section of the definitive sale agreement, a seller may be required to provide funds to the buyer for any accrued employee vacation time as of the closing date, or to pay such funds directly to employees as of the closing date. Similarly, a seller may be required to pay some or all of the employee severance costs incurred as a result of the transaction.)

- **Absence of material adverse changes and operations conducted in the ordinary course**. Sellers will generally also be asked to represent that the business has suffered no material adverse change since the date of the last audited balance sheet, and that it has been and will continue to be operated in the ordinary course of business between the date of the last audited balance sheet and the closing date. This means, for example, that there have been no unusual dividends paid, no unusual salary increases made, no unusual contracts entered into, or extraordinary capital commitments made.

- **Other representations.** In addition to those discussed above, a seller is commonly asked to make other representations such as the following:

1. All tax returns of the corporation are correct and all taxes due have been paid.

2. The corporation has the right to do business in each jurisdiction in which it operates.

3. The business has the right to use any trade names, trademarks, and other proprietary rights it uses in conducting its operations.

4. There is no outstanding or threatened litigation against the company, other than claims identified on a specified schedule.

5. Except where noted on an attached schedule, the business has not been operated in violation of any governmental law or regulation.

6. The company has no undisclosed liabilities incurred outside the ordinary course of business.

7. The company has good title to the assets being sold.

8. All equipment being purchased is in good operating condition (ordinary wear and tear excepted), all inventory being purchased is merchantable, and all buildings being purchased are structurally sound.

9. The seller has made all material contracts available for review, and the company is in compliance with each of them.

10. The company has had no material labor relations problems except as disclosed on a separate schedule.

11. The company has good relationships with its customers, suppliers, and other third parties, and is not aware of the potential loss of any customer whose loss would have a material adverse impact on the business.

12. There are no material misstatements or omissions contained in the seller's representations (a so-called "10b-5" representation).

FORM OF REPRESENTATIONS: "ABSOLUTE" VERSUS "KNOWLEDGE." Buyers like representations to be made on an "absolute" basis or without qualification. This means that, even if a seller contends that he was unaware of a violation, he is liable for damages that a buyer may suffer as a result of a representation being breached. Representations may be qualified by prefacing them with the phrase "to the knowledge of" the seller. Then a buyer needs to prove that the seller had knowledge of an environmental contamination problem, for example, before it can collect from the seller.

It is common for definitive sale agreements to have a combination of absolute and knowledge representations. For example, it would be customary to give absolute representations on such things as the accuracy of financial statements, having good title to all property, payment of all taxes, and the absence of any outstanding litigation. On the other hand, it is not uncommon for a seller to qualify "to his knowledge" such representations as the business having been operated in compliance with all applicable laws and regulations.

The rationale for qualifying such a representation is that, while a seller might believe the business is in full compliance with all laws and regulations, due to the complexity of the matter, there are likely to be a number of violations (particularly minor violations) of which even the most diligent of sellers will not be aware. Rather than risk getting tripped up on this, he makes the representation based on his actual knowledge.

Buyers like to get as many of the representations as possible made on an absolute basis rather than just on the basis of knowledge, because an absolute representation provides the buyer with greater protection against unexpected losses after the closing. Several years ago, I negotiated a transaction for a buyer in which we asked for and received an absolute representation from the sellers that there were no threatened losses of customer accounts that would have a material adverse impact on the overall operation of the business.

Shortly after the closing, the business lost a key account (which accounted for at least 10 percent of total sales). After an extensive investigation, we found that the company had received a letter from the departing customer prior to the closing stating that it planned to shift its purchases to another firm. While the owner responsible for sales insisted he had not known about the letter, we were still able to get a significant payment from the sellers as damages for the lost business because the representation was made on an "absolute" rather than a "knowledge" basis.

INDEMNIFICATION

Indemnification is the procedure by which a buyer seeks to collect damages from a seller for losses arising out of breach by a seller of its representations and warranties contained in the definitive sale agreement, and by which a buyer may shift responsibility to a seller for third-party claims and other losses arising out of the operation of the business prior to closing. The latter is commonly referred to as "watch-to-watch" indemnification.

The term "watch-to-watch" stems from the Navy, where the officer in charge at a given time is responsible for any problem that occurs when he is on duty, or during his "watch." In business parlance, it refers to the period of ownership. It is the seller's watch until the closing occurs, and then the buyer's watch begins. Thus, it is not uncommon to have the seller's indemnification cover third-party claims and other losses arising out of the operation of the business prior to the closing, regardless of whether the events or conditions giving rise to the claims or losses constituted a breach by the seller of its representations or warranties.

For example, if six months after the closing a company recalls defective products that were made prior to the closing, the cost of that recall would be borne by the seller, assuming that the definitive sale agreement contained a "watch-to-watch" indemnification provision. The defective product was made when the seller owned the business, so he would be responsible for any problems that occur with that product. Obviously, the buyer would be responsible for problems that occur once his period of ownership begins, unless he can prove they were the result of something that stems from, or can be traced back to, a pre-closing event.

In addition to describing the specific matters to be covered by the seller's indemnification, the section on indemnification in the definitive sale agreement usually sets forth various limitations on the buyer's right to seek indemnification from the seller, such as:

- How long the indemnification will run (other than what the statute of limitations under the laws governing the contract may provide).

- The cap on the amount of damages for which a seller could be liable.

- Whether the damages will run from the first dollar suffered or whether there will be a level of damages that must be reached before any amount is paid.

- Whether a portion of the purchase price will be escrowed to cover indemnification claims.

- Whether all sellers will share equally in the payment of damages or whether one seller might be required to step up if one of the other sellers does not have the financial wherewithal to do so.

The following sections cover each of these items beginning with the last one.

"JOINT AND SEVERAL" VERSUS "SEVERAL." If there is a single seller, he usually is responsible for indemnifying the buyer for the entirety of all covered losses. The matter is complicated, however, when there are two or more owners. Let us assume that there are three sellers who each own a third of the business that is being sold. Ideally from the seller's standpoint, each of the three sellers would be liable only for a pro-rata portion (i.e., one-third) of any amount collected under the indemnification. This would be liability on a "several" basis.

If, for example, a claim was successfully made for $150,000, each of the three sellers ideally would be liable for paying $50,000. That works well as long as each has the funds to pay his share of the claim. Problems for the buyer arise, however, if one or more of the sellers does not have the funds available to pay his share of the claim. If the buyer has to collect from each seller separately, and if one of the sellers does not have the funds to pay the buyer, the buyer is out that portion of the claim.

As a way of covering such potential situations, buyers will sometimes insist that the sellers agree to indemnify the buyer for losses on a "joint and several" basis. This means that, if one or more of the sellers do not have funds to pay their percentage of the claim comparable to their percentage of ownership, any one of the remaining sellers is liable to pay off the entire claim. The same is true if the buyer simply determines that it is not convenient to pursue each seller for his pro-rata portion of the claim. Literally, each seller is responsible for up to 100 percent of the entire claim.

At first glance, this may seem unfair, but consider the following. If a father started the business, still owns most of the stock, but has provided other members of his family with small amounts of stock, a buyer does not want to have to track down several small shareholders for their respective shares of the claim. Instead, the buyer wants to be able to go to a single party, in this case the principal owner, and serve him with notice for the full amount. The principal owner, in turn, can turn to his family members to share in paying the claim.

ESCROW ACCOUNTS. To minimize problems that might arise if one or more shareholders lacks funds to pay for a claim, some buyers will require that a portion of the selling price be placed in an escrow account for a period of time following the closing. For example, 10 percent of the purchase price might be placed in an escrow account for a period of 12 to 24 months (long enough to get through one full audit cycle following the closing). Usually the escrow funds are placed in an interest-bearing account.

Practice varies regarding the treatment of interest. Sometimes the interest income follows the principal. This means that, if part of the escrow funds are paid to the buyer to satisfy a claim, the buyer also receives a corresponding portion of the interest, while the seller gets the rest of the escrow money along with the remaining interest income. Alternatively, the escrow provisions might stipulate that the buyer is entitled to be reimbursed out of the escrow only for the actual amount of his losses. If that is the case, the seller would receive all interest earned on the escrowed funds, unless the principal is insufficient to reimburse the buyer for the full amount of his losses.

DOLLAR CAP ON THE AMOUNT. Without a cap on the amount of funds that may be collected under the indemnification, a seller could be liable for an unlimited amount of money, even more than the proceeds received from the sale. Such an event could happen if a major environmental clean-up problem were to occur, for example. To protect a seller against that contingency, most definitive sale agreements place a cap on the dollar amount that a buyer can potentially collect from a seller with respect to most claims.

I have never seen a cap exceed the selling price, and the lowest cap I have seen was 5 percent of the purchase price (which equaled the amount of the proceeds placed in escrow). In the latter case, this enabled the sellers to know up front that they would never have to come up with funds not already in escrow to satisfy a potential claim. From my experience, I would say it is common to cap the indemnity at 25 to 50 percent of the purchase price for most sales. But, in some instances, the cap may run higher (such as up to the purchase price) for something like environmental matters, especially where it is known that a location has been polluted with hazardous substances. In addition, in a few cases (such as good title to property, tax liabilities, breach of covenant, and fraud), there may be no cap whatsoever on the amount of the seller's potential liability.

BASKETS. Because paying a succession of claims for minimal amounts is administratively burdensome, most definitive sale agreements provide a threshold or deductible amount (commonly referred to as a "basket") below which claims (other than, typically, those excluded from the cap) are not paid. For example, the basket for paying claims might be $100,000 for a $20 million transaction (½ of 1 percent of the selling price). This means that if all claims do not total $100,000 during the indemnity period, no claims are paid. If, however, claims exceed $100,000, then the seller may be required to pay back to the first dollar of claims made, in which case the basket serves as a threshold.

Alternatively, the claims amount may not go back to the first dollar. In such a case, the basket serves as a pure deductible; if claims are sustained in excess of $100,000 (in this example), the seller would effectively have a $100,000 increase in his proceeds and the buyer would have a price increase of the same amount.

Whether I am advising clients on the sell or the buy side, I feel that once the dollar level of the basket is reached, the seller should be liable for claims back to the first dollar of claims.

LENGTH OF TERM. The length of the term that the indemnification (as well as any underlying representations or warranties) will run should also be fixed in the definitive sale agreement. If the term is not specified in the contract, it normally will be whatever the statute of limitations is for the state whose laws are to govern the document. But since statutes of limitations vary from state to state and among events, the parties are usually well advised to specify for themselves time limits for key items in the definitive sale agreement.

Most sellers feel it would be overly onerous to have the indemnification run for a term as extended as the statute of limitations, so most contracts specify a shorter period for the survival of many of the seller's indemnification obligations. It would not be uncommon, for example, for the indemnity period to be two or three years for breach of most representations and warranties, including the accuracy of financial statements, the affirmation that the business has been operated in its ordinary manner prior to the sale, and the assurance that the buyer has the right to use the trademarks and trade names employed in the business.

The seller's indemnification may run to the statute of limitations for things such as good title to property, tax liabilities, breach of covenant, and fraud. In rare instances the definitive sale agreement may include an indemnification that runs even longer than the statute of limitations (e.g., indemnification for breach of the environmental representation), so long as it is not prevented under the laws of the state governing the definitive sale agreement. Where a selling company has a plant that has disposed of some hazardous waste substances on the site, a buyer may insist on an extended period of indemnification to make sure that all remedial action is completed before the indemnity expires.

ADJUSTMENTS TO THE PURCHASE PRICE
AFTER THE CLOSING

Just as there can be adjustments to the purchase price between the time the definitive sale agreement is signed and the closing, there also can be post-closing purchase price adjustments. Two of the more common are an adjustment based on a change in the balance sheet and one based on a change in operating results.

POST-CLOSING ADJUSTMENTS TO THE BALANCE SHEET. Most purchase prices are based on the balance sheet. If there is a change, either upward or downward, in the value of the assets, the purchase price is adjusted upward or downward, as I have previously discussed. Most closing-date balance sheets, however, are not based on the actual inventory, receivables, payables, and accrued liabilities as of the closing date, since the value of these items typically varies on a daily basis. Rather, the business is sold based on the **estimated** values as of the closing date, which are then "trued-up" within 30 or 60 days after the closing. The adjustment to the purchase price may be up or down, and a check is then paid to either the seller or the buyer according to the difference in the amount projected at the closing and the actual amount determined later.

In several transactions on which I have worked, we actually did a true balance sheet (as opposed to an estimate) as of the closing date so we did not have to provide for a post-closing price adjustment. We did this by having accountants come in a few days before the closing date to determine the accounts receivable, payables, and accrued liabilities and update them daily right up to the closing date. Then, while the business was closed on the weekend prior to the closing (Friday evening and Saturday), we took a full inventory. On Sunday, we added up all the numbers for each location being sold, and were ready to close on Monday morning with an accurate balance sheet for the business. I have seen this procedure work effectively for numerous transactions—even for one involving more than 50 locations and where grain inventory had to be physically weighed at many of them!

There is often an advantage to the seller in preparing the closing-date balance sheet this way, in that the key accounting people at each location are still employees of the seller. Once the closing takes place, employee loyalties tend to shift to the buyer, and the buyer will have time to ask his new employees to look for ways to seek price adjustments in his favor before the post-closing financial statement is completed.

I have seen arguments on post-closing adjustments go on for months after the time specified for their resolution had passed. Thus, when selling a business, I usually encourage the seller to have the final balance sheet prepared prior to the closing to avoid a post-closing price adjustment. Such post-closing adjustments almost invariably cost the seller and reduce the price for a buyer.

POST-CLOSING ADJUSTMENTS BASED ON PERFORMANCE. In some instances, a buyer agrees to pay a certain price for a business based on a predetermined level of earnings being achieved during the balance of the year. The definitive sale agreement may then provide that, if that level of earnings is not achieved, the seller will remit a certain amount to the buyer—perhaps the amount by which the earnings fell short **times** the same multiple of earnings that the buyer paid for the business. Likewise, the sale agreement may provide that if the earnings exceed the specified amount, the buyer will pay the seller an additional amount equal to the amount by which earnings exceeded the specified level **times** the same multiple of earnings the buyer paid for the business.

Before a seller agrees to such a post-closing performance adjustment, he should be pretty confident that the projected earnings level will be achieved or else satisfied that, if the purchase price is reduced by the maximum amount possible, the remaining purchase price will still be acceptable. In addition, if the buyer and seller decide to use a performance adjustment, they need to prepare a budget and procedures for operating the business between the closing and the end of the performance adjustment period—and make them a part of the agreements signed at or prior to the closing.

GOVERNING LAW AND JURISDICTION

Most definitive sale agreements specify a state whose laws will govern the document if claims are filed; lawyers often refer to this as a "choice of law" provision. The buyer typically seeks to have the state in which his company is based as the one whose laws will govern the agreement, while the seller usually prefers the state in which his business is headquartered. Each tends to prefer his own state's law because he (or at least his lawyers) is familiar with that law and the manner in which the definitive sale agreement is likely to be interpreted under that state's law.

Usually the buyer's wishes will prevail in selecting the state whose laws will govern. However, when the buyer and seller cannot agree on which state to specify for the governing law, the agreement may remain silent on the issue. If the contract is silent and the parties are from different states, courts will typically assess various factors to determine which governing law should apply.

A related issue is the jurisdiction (i.e., which state or federal courts) in which claims and any litigation related to the definitive sale agreement are to be filed; lawyers often refer to this as a "choice of forum" provision. The definitive sale agreement may specify that claims are to be filed in the state courts of a particular state. If the buyer and the seller are from different states, federal courts may also be used. Again, the buyer will generally prefer to have cases handled in the jurisdiction in which it is headquartered. On the other hand, the seller may feel that a judge or jury will be more sympathetic in the state where the business is based, and thus will try to get the venue there.

The buyer and the seller may compromise by agreeing to submit claims to the non-exclusive jurisdiction of the state or federal courts sitting in the state in which the buyer is headquartered. This gives either party some flexibility in deciding whether to file any claim it may have in state or federal court, and also enables the party being sued to ask that a case be moved to another court if it thinks that is important.

Finally, contracts occasionally include a mandatory arbitration or mediation clause under which both parties agree that disputes will be arbitrated or mediated before, or in lieu of, filing a claim in court. Arbitration or mediation is often seen as a cheaper and more expedient method of handling disputes, and thus may be advantageous for both a seller and a buyer.

CHAPTER TEN

NEGOTIATING OTHER AGREEMENTS

While the definitive sale agreement is the most important and comprehensive of the legal documents relating to a sale, there usually are other legal agreements that are negotiated at the same time.

For example, if an entrepreneur retains ownership of certain offices or other facilities used by the business being sold, then a real estate lease agreement also has to be negotiated and entered into with the buyer. It is important that a seller retain a real estate attorney to be part of the negotiations on the lease. Beyond determining a competitive lease rate and the length of the lease, there will be several other items that the lease should address. For example, who will be responsible for which repairs to the facilities? Who will be responsible for any environmental clean-ups? And, who will be responsible for any personal or building-related litigation that might occur?

A TRANSITION SERVICES AGREEMENT

When another firm buys a business, it may not be prepared to take over the operations in total as of the closing date. If a larger corporation spins off one of its operations, for example, the buyer may want the selling company to continue providing certain services for a few months. If a centralized computer has been used to prepare the monthly financial statements, for example, the buyer may need a few months to convert the operation to its own computer or install an independent system in the purchased operation.

Other corporate services that the buyer may need from the seller for a period after the closing might include payroll preparation and some record keeping for employee benefits. Sometimes the business that is sold has office space in the selling corporation's facilities, and the buyer may need to rent the space until its offices can be relocated to new facilities.

When an entrepreneur sells a freestanding business, there may be less need for a transition services agreement or fewer items to be covered. Still, one is often needed. I recently negotiated the sale of a freestanding business for an entrepreneur; under the terms of the sale, the seller's management entered into an agreement to continue to operate the business for 90 days after the closing. So, they entered into a transition services agreement that covered what personnel, accounting, and computer services would be provided, for how long, and at what cost. It worked well, and at the end of the transition services period, the seller moved on to a consulting relationship with the buyer.

Just as the scope of services to be performed under a transition services agreement will vary from one sale to another, so will the term for which the services are provided. The typical period for transition services to be rendered after a closing ranges from three to six months. The period has to be long enough for the buyer to put in place the resources to take over the services the seller is providing under the transition services agreement, but usually neither the buyer nor the seller will want to make the term longer than is necessary to complete the transition. On rare occasions, when the initially agreed-upon time proves too short, the transition services agreement may be extended for 30 days, for example, to complete the changeover.

With respect to compensation for a transition services agreement, if a selling corporation is providing the services, usually the cost is close to the company's actual cost for providing the service. This would include its actual rent and related expenses if space is being provided. In the case of services performed by individuals, it would include the actual cost of the persons involved in providing services (including their compensation, employee benefits costs, the pro-rata share of their office space and the cost of their utilities, and other overhead).

If an entrepreneur has sold a business and the buyer looks to him to personally provide certain transition services, he should also price them to cover his full costs. If his management counsel is to be provided for a short period, his compensation needs to be priced on the basis of the amount of time required of him each week multiplied by a competitive salary for such a role. Usually the terms for this will be covered in a separate employment or consulting agreement.

An Employment or Consulting Agreement

It is quite common for the seller of a business to enter into an employment or consulting agreement with the buyer for a period of time after the closing. This is often a mutually desirable agreement, with the buyer wanting to be able to call on the seller for counsel about the business after the closing and the seller having an interest in getting additional income after the sale.

The term of such agreements generally varies from one to three years, depending on how involved the buyer wants the seller to be. It is also possible to have a longer-term contract during which the amount of time involved gradually declines. For example, a seller may be available on a full-time basis for six months following the closing, half-time for the next six months, and then a day or two a month for another two years. Usually after six months to a year both the seller and the buyer will desire less than full-time involvement from the seller. The buyer generally wants to assume control of the business and rely less on the seller, and a seller will prefer to move the focus of his life to other activities, especially since the buyer will be making the critical decisions.

It is important for the buyer and the seller to agree on the amount of time the seller is to commit to the business after the closing, so the seller knows what flexibility he will have in planning his schedule. If less than full time is going to be required, especially after the initial six months or so, I try to have the amount of time the buyer requires of the seller stated as so many hours or days a month, with the provision that the buyer and seller will work out a mutually acceptable schedule for each month in advance. This gives a seller the opportunity to plan for extensive travel or other activities, knowing that he will have extended periods of time during which he can do other things.

While most sellers will not be involved in their businesses on a full-time basis for an extended period after the closing, there are, of course, exceptions. Some large companies purchase businesses with the provision that the selling owner and his key associates retain their management positions for at least three to five years after the closing, for example. In such situations, the buyer is purchasing the business, at least in part, because the management of the company being sold has done a superior job of running the business and made it an attractive investment for the buyer. The buyer thus wants to retain the management in place for an extended period.

Warren Buffet of Berkshire Hathaway has purchased many smaller businesses from entrepreneurs with the proviso that the sellers continue to run their former businesses. In such instances it is important to have a written understanding between the buyer and the seller about how the business will be managed after the closing, how much authority the seller and his management team will have in making decisions, and in which instances the buyer will need to be consulted before final decisions are made.

A related issue that should also be specified in an employee or consulting agreement is to whom the seller will report during the term of the agreement. If the seller is to have major responsibilities in running the business or otherwise be actively involved in the business—even as a consultant—it is important to know to whom he will report. I always believe that a seller should report to a decision-maker as high in the buyer's organization as possible. It is important that the person to whom the seller reports be a decision-maker; otherwise the seller's input and recommendations may not get to those responsible for making decisions. A seller who has led a life of making decisions can quickly become very frustrated if he cannot interact directly with another decision-maker on an ongoing basis.

Finally, there is the issue of compensation. Once the responsibilities a seller is to perform after the closing have been determined, as well as how much time is likely to be required for performing them, it is appropriate to turn to the issue of compensation for these services. If it is an employment contract for full-time executive services, compensation should be comparable to the market for such positions. It should include a base salary and a bonus sufficient to provide a good incentive. If the buyer is a public company, it would also be appropriate to get stock options in the parent company, as well as other benefits that the buyer provides to its executives with comparable responsibilities.

If the responsibilities are more of a consulting nature, the contract may provide for a daily rate. A daily rate should be fairly liberal because, when the buyer calls the seller for advice, it will likely be for counsel on rather important issues, with potentially large dollar implications for the buyer. As an alternative to a daily rate, I generally prefer a monthly retainer. I have found that, after an initial transition period, the seller usually is not called on as often as both parties originally had expected. Thus, a monthly retainer generally results in more income for the seller than a daily rate paid for actual days worked.

A NON-COMPETE AGREEMENT

Another agreement that probably will be negotiated at the same time the definitive sale agreement is prepared is the non-compete agreement. A buyer who pays a fair price for a business does not want the seller to go out into the marketplace and start a competing business—or to work for or invest in one—for a period of time after the closing. Non-compete periods vary from state to state, and also from industry to industry. My experience has been that many run for three years, with most starting on the closing date. In some instances, however, a buyer will insist that, if the seller continues to work in the business, there be a non-compete period starting with the date he leaves the business, if it is of his own volition. This period may be shorter, such as a year or two.

While a buyer generally would like to get as long a non-compete period as possible from a seller, the buyer needs to keep in mind that courts have ruled it unfair for a non-compete agreement to deprive an individual of the opportunity to make a fair living. Some courts have ruled that such an agreement cannot be more than three years. In certain instances, even three years has been ruled too long.

A non-compete agreement also should specify the products and services, as well as the geographic area, to be covered. Usually, the geographic area will be the area in which the selling company currently operates. The products and services covered will usually be those the company currently makes and those that are planned. Sometimes the product or service category is broadened a little to assure the buyer that the seller also will not enter closely allied areas. Non-compete agreements nearly always also forbid a seller from seeking business from former customers during the term of the agreement. Finally, non-compete agreements often preclude a seller from soliciting employees to work for him in another business.

Additional compensation is usually not paid for a non-compete agreement, but a buyer may request that part of the purchase price be allocated to this agreement. This is usually done for tax considerations, because the portion of the selling price that is allocated to the non-compete agreement can be written off as a tax deduction over the life of the agreement. If the non-compete agreement is for three years, for example, the portion of the purchase price that is allocated to the agreement can be written off over the three-year period, reducing taxes accordingly. That portion of the purchase price that is goodwill, on the other hand, has to be written off over 15 years for tax purposes. The shorter write-off period for a non-compete agreement (instead of the longer period for writing off regular goodwill) will enhance short-term cash flow and thus benefit the buyer.

A seller, on the other hand, generally would prefer that none of the purchase price be allocated to the non-compete agreement. This is because he usually will have to pay ordinary income tax on the amount assigned to the non-compete agreement, while he could use the lower capital gains tax rate on any amount assigned to goodwill. Sometimes buyers and sellers resolve this tax issue with the buyer agreeing to pay a higher total purchase price but getting to allocate to the non-compete agreement as large a part of purchase price as the IRS is likely to accept as reasonable.

WHEN A FAIRNESS OPINION MAY BE USED

When a publicly traded company buys or sells a relatively large business, it may decide to get a "fairness opinion." A fairness opinion is a letter addressed to the company's board of directors or its shareholders that is usually issued by its investment banker. Its purpose is to state to the board or the shareholders that the investment banking firm has reviewed the terms of the proposed purchase or sale and that—based on its knowledge of other similar transactions that have been completed recently—the investment banking firm deems the proposed purchase or sale price and other key terms to be "fair" for the company requesting the opinion. It is done to reassure a firm's board of directors that the company has received a fair price if it is selling a business, or is paying a fair price if it is buying a company.

About the only time an entrepreneur encounters a request for a fairness opinion is (1) if the business he is selling is quite large and could have a material impact on the operating performance or balance sheet of the acquiring company and (2) if the acquiring company is publicly traded. In each case the acquiring company will be expected to pay for the cost of obtaining the fairness opinion since the opinion is being issued for its benefit. The only risk to the seller of a buyer seeking to get a fairness opinion is that—if the issuing investment banker should feel the price is excessive or that the acquisition will have an adverse impact on the buyer's income statement or balance sheet—it could lead to either a reduced purchase price or a cessation of negotiations.

CHAPTER ELEVEN

BASIC PRINCIPLES OF GOOD NEGOTIATING

In the last few chapters, I discussed the key components involved in negotiating the sale of a business. These included (1) deciding which firm to go with and trying to get its offer enhanced as much as possible; (2) negotiating the basic terms of the sale, such as price and form of payment; and (3) negotiating the legal documents typically involved in a sale. These activities take considerable time and usually involve extensive negotiations.

During my years of leading negotiations on the purchase and sale of numerous businesses, I have concluded that there is an art to successful negotiating. Based on my experiences, I have compiled several fundamental principles for negotiating, which I have grouped into three categories: creating the right setting, developing the right negotiating strategies, and conducting good negotiations.

CREATING THE RIGHT SETTING

1. **<u>Provide Adequate Time When Setting Meeting Dates</u>.**
   When setting dates for negotiating sessions, make sure that
   everyone who will be involved blocks out adequate time on
   his calendar. Assess what should be sufficient time to accomplish the task—and then try to hold open an extra day as a
   safety factor. For example, if the group generally feels that two
   days should be adequate to negotiate a definitive sale
   agreement, block out a third day on everyone's schedule to
   accommodate any unexpected delays.

   It is usually easier to stay on an extra day and complete a task
   than to reschedule another session later. And, with many
   people involved, it is usually easier to get a commitment to
   blocking out the "extra time" when the original arrangements
   are made than it will be later when it becomes clear that not
   enough time has been set aside.

2. **<u>Provide a Comfortable Meeting Environment</u>.** The team
   hosting the negotiations should provide a comfortable
   environment with appropriate amenities. While sometimes a
   sterile room with hard seats and no meal or beverage service
   is conducive to reaching agreement on a "sticky" issue,
   usually you will create a more positive mood for reaching
   accord by having soft comfortable chairs (with arms), coffee
   and soft drinks (with plenty of ice), and meal service
   provided on a timely basis.

   Always pick a room large enough to accommodate additional
   people who may be brought in during the session, and provide
   a separate room for one side to caucus separately. It is also
   important to make sure that good ventilation is provided in
   the meeting room(s). If the meeting is likely to continue into
   the evening, it may be necessary to notify the building manager
   to leave the air conditioning, air blowers, or heat turned on
   after regular hours.

3. **Set Daily Objectives.** The negotiating teams should begin each day by agreeing on loose objectives that both sides would like to accomplish before the end of the day. Concurrent with this, ascertain how long each player will be available that day so that if someone has to leave early, appropriate issues involving that person can be addressed prior to his departure.

I have found that agreeing on a general agenda at the start of the day usually gives the negotiating teams more common expectations for the day—and thus enables them to accomplish more by the time they adjourn—than if the discussions just evolve without common objectives. It also minimizes surprises that can occur later in the day if someone's need to leave early has not previously been communicated to the other side.

4. **Be Willing to Continue Negotiations into the Evening.** Some of the best negotiations occur between 7 P.M. and 10 P.M.—especially if not as much progress has been made during the day as both parties had hoped for based on their previously set agenda for the day. Then, as the hour becomes late and parties on both sides begin to tire, they are often more prone to compromise.

5. **Have Appropriate Staff Available to Work Late.** If you want effective negotiations to continue into the evening, you may have to make appropriate arrangements. For example, people should be available to retype drafts, make copies, and coordinate meal and beverage service. It is often helpful, if possible, for the law firm hosting the negotiations on the definitive sale agreement to arrange for overnight retyping of a draft with revisions agreed upon during the day, so both parties can review a new draft when they gather the following morning.

DEVELOPING THE RIGHT NEGOTIATING STRATEGIES

1. **Anticipate Potential Problems and Develop Contingency Plans.** The seller's team should try to anticipate anything that may go awry during a given day in the negotiating process, and try to have contingency plans ready to use if needed. It is always good to anticipate what the other side may ask for and the logic its team will use to rationalize each request. Then, in advance of the discussions, you can think through how you would respond, so you will have good arguments ready if they are needed.

2. **Always Try to Be Reasonable During Negotiations.** A good negotiator listens carefully in order to ascertain what is important to the other side. Try to find a way to give the other side as much as possible on the items it deems most critical, while holding firm for the items most important to your side. Never be reluctant to give in on some things that are not critical to your side, so that you have a better chance of getting the things that are most important to you. Never try to win on all the issues. Those who try to keep negotiations between the 40-yard-lines of a football field will usually end up getting their way more often than those who constantly try to "beat" their opponents on every issue.

    Remember, no deal is worthwhile unless both sides feel good about it. While it is fine to have a reputation for being a tough negotiator, you also want to be known as someone who is considered to be fair in negotiations. In the final analysis, a reputation for honesty and fairness is the most important asset each of us has.

3. **Be Prepared to "Walk" on Critical Issues.** While you should always try to be reasonable, that does not mean you should give in to the other side most of the time. If a buyer believes an owner really has to sell his business, he will continuously try to extract concessions. But, if a prospective

buyer wants very much to purchase a company and knows that several issues are "walk points" for the owner, and if the owner's representatives hold firm on those positions (even if the owner really does need to sell his company), then the owner's team will usually enhance its negotiating position.

This position is further enhanced if the seller gives in on other "non-walk" issues as discussions proceed. It is surprising how frequently a bridge can be built to accommodate both sides when each side seeks to find the other side's key "walk issues." In most negotiations, the items (excluding price) most important to one side are not the items most important to the other side; recognizing that fact facilitates compromise.

CONDUCTING GOOD NEGOTIATIONS

1. **<u>Emphasize Resolving Immediate Problems</u>.** When faced with difficulty in negotiating serious issues with a potential buyer, try to solve only the immediate problems of the current day. Do not worry about the problems that loom on the horizon. If each day's problems are successfully addressed, the larger issues will get solved in due time.

Several years ago, I was coordinating the acquisition of a business that would provide the company for which I worked with an excellent base in a new area. It was a highly sought-after business, with lots of firms bidding on it. Our company ultimately ended up being the selected bidder—not because we made the highest bid, but because we had come within 5 percent of the highest bid and had then demonstrated that we would provide a better home for the management and employees.

The process that followed—very tense and extended contract negotiations—was filled with one huge hurdle after another. Throughout the entire process I took the attitude that I would try to deal only with the problems at hand during a given day and not worry about or focus on the hurdles that I knew lay ahead. If we looked at the overall picture, it appeared to be a virtually impossible task. So, instead, we dissected the overall project into numerous items, and then each day focused only on the issues that needed to be dealt with that day. Day by day we dealt with a huge number of issues in this manner and ultimately completed the entire transaction very successfully.

2. **Use Teamwork.** A good negotiator never tries to analyze, negotiate, or finalize a transaction single-handedly; teamwork minimizes mistakes. Teamwork also fosters a broader sense of ownership among those with whom you are working, which is usually critical to the successful consummation of a sale.

During my years of negotiating I have often gained much insight and good information by relying on specialists in a variety of functional areas. For example, when it comes to negotiating items in a definitive sale agreement that involve human resources, I have found it very useful to have specialists who can advise me on the intricacies of this functional area. This area has lots of complexities, including weighing potential liabilities for employee claims, determining adequate funding of benefit programs, deciding which party is responsible for workers' compensation claims, and making the proper calculation of vacation and sick-leave accruals. There also are countless government regulations that require compliance in human resources; an expert in this area can be invaluable in assuring that these have been properly handled.

The same can be said about the importance of using functional experts in other areas, such as taxes, accounting, and environmental matters. When an expert in each specialized area signs off on those portions of the definitive sale agreement about which he has expertise, the team negotiator knows that he has a better overall agreement, because the team negotiator simply cannot know the best way to handle every issue in each functional area. Backed by information from functional specialists, he becomes a much more effective negotiator.

3. **Have Periodic Team Caucuses.** Never hesitate to call a caucus with your fellow team members if doubt exists about the best way to respond to a proposal made by the other side. Hopefully, a caucus will facilitate agreement on the best way to respond and the best arguments to use in delivering the response. Again, a negotiator can often gain different insights from his fellow team members by taking periodic breaks to seek their input. Sometimes another team member will have observed reactions from the other side that the negotiator has missed, and that teammate may have constructive suggestions on how to respond. Other team members may also have additional helpful inputs or arguments that will assist the negotiator in determining the best way to proceed.

4. **Use Small Groups to Resolve "Sticky" Issues.** Oftentimes, if each side has several members sitting in on negotiations, a "grandstanding" environment is created, whereby the flavor of the dialogue can take on more show than substance. Then, it may be advantageous for a smaller group of one or two persons from each side to meet with their counterpart(s) in a relaxed setting in which they can thoughtfully try to work out an accord. This gets the key players away from the emotionalism that is often created in a larger setting and lets them listen more effectively to the key concerns of the other side.

Subgroups also can be effective in dealing with specific issues that the broad group need not focus on. For example, tax specialists might focus on reaching agreement on how the purchase price should be allocated; they are the ones best equipped to do this and need not take the time of the full negotiating group. Their recommendations should be brought back to the full group for clarification questions and the larger group's "blessing."

5. **Consider Grouping Proposed Compromises.** In seeking to resolve tough issues that are in dispute, it is often better to try to put all the open issues and alternative positions on the table collectively, and then attempt to develop a proposed package solution for the open issues together, rather than dealing with individual issues separately. This process of putting several issues into a common basket can be referred to as "basket negotiations."

Putting six or eight remaining issues into a proposed basket solution frequently enables both sides to get acceptable trade-offs. By facilitating compromise it also usually speeds up negotiations. Remember that the issues most important to one side are usually not the same issues that are most important to the other side, so trade-offs made in a basket approach may be easier to accept than they would be if each issue were dealt with separately. Putting a few remaining issues into a basket for resolution may also help prevent "ratcheting up" negotiations, whereby one side keeps "taking" what the other side will give on each issue without compromising proportionately.

When presenting a basket of solutions to the other side, it is important to state that the basket contains some of the positions each side has advocated, and that the other side will, therefore, like some of the solutions but probably not all of them. Whoever presents the basket then needs to make it clear to the other side that it cannot cherry-pick among the proposals; the proposals need to be accepted or rejected as a group. If your team has done a good job of assessing what is most important to each side and has tried to present a balanced basket in which both sides get key components of what they want, the basket approach can be useful in resolving remaining issues.

I have found that following the basic attributes of this list of negotiating principles generally leads to successful negotiations.

CHAPTER TWELVE

PREPARING FOR THE CLOSING

OPERATING THE BUSINESS BETWEEN THE SIGNING AND THE CLOSING

Once the definitive sale agreement and related agreements have been negotiated and signed, attention turns to operating the business until the closing, and preparing for the closing itself.

CONTRACTUAL LIMITATIONS ON THE SCOPE OF ACTIVITIES THAT MAY BE CONDUCTED. The definitive sale agreement will generally stipulate the manner in which the business can be operated between the signing and the closing. In a nutshell, generally all activities need to be conducted in the ordinary course of business, unless otherwise provided for in the contract.

Usually, this means that there can be no special or unusual dividends or cash distributions to shareholders, no raises to employees beyond what has traditionally been given, and no unusual capital expenditures or capital commitments. Generally the definitive sale agreement will specify a dollar amount above which the buyer must give its approval for new contracts or commitments to be made. This enables the seller to propose new commitments that he feels are appropriate, but they will require the sign-off of the buyer before consummation.

EMPHASIZING COLLECTION OF RECEIVABLES. Generally, the seller will have to guarantee the collectability of all receivables on the books at the closing. The buyer will receive payments toward many of them after the closing in the ordinary course of business (particularly from those accounts that are current in their payments). But, as discussed earlier, the buyer will not have any special incentive to try to collect old accounts receivable, since he will get a payment back from the seller at a later date for whatever amount of receivables he does not collect.

A seller, therefore, should do everything in his power between the signing and the closing to collect any accounts receivable that are not current. If there are receivables that are 60 to 90 days old, for example, the seller should go after these aggressively, including making an offer to discount them if they are paid promptly. Once the closing occurs, the seller will have no real means of collecting them, and those who owe the business money will probably be less inclined to pay a former owner.

MANAGING CASH. While it will vary from transaction to transaction, most sales agreements will permit the seller to "sweep" the company's cash to his own account as of the closing date—at least any cash above the level needed to run the business in the ordinary course of events. In most transactions, an adjustment will be made to the purchase price at or after closing to bring the purchase price in line with any change in the value of the assets and liabilities between the date of the balance sheet used when the definitive sale agreement is signed and the closing date balance sheet.

In such instances, whether the level of cash is high or low at the closing date will not affect the proceeds to the seller. However, in some stock sales, there is no adjustment to the purchase price at the closing for a change in the value of the assets or liabilities between the signing and the closing. In such cases, a seller would want to build up as much cash as possible before the closing in order to enhance the proceeds received—assuming the definitive agreement gives him the right to sweep the cash above a certain level.

MAKING SURE A MATERIAL ADVERSE CHANGE CLAUSE IS NOT TRIGGERED. Most definitive sale agreements have a provision that the purchase price can be re-negotiated by the buyer—and in some instances that the transaction can even be cancelled by the buyer—if a "material adverse change" occurs in the business between the time of signing and the closing. Examples would be the loss of a major customer that accounts for over 10 percent of sales, or the drop-off in sales and earnings of more than a specified amount. It really is important that a seller make all reasonable efforts to keep the business operating strongly during the interim period to minimize the chance of triggering a material adverse change clause.

COMPLETING THE DUE DILIGENCE PROCESS

While a buyer usually will have completed most of its due diligence activities before signing the definitive sale agreement, there is generally some additional due diligence done between the signing and the closing. The buyer will want to monitor ongoing developments in the business—not only interim financial results, but also the overall state of the business he is purchasing. In addition, it is common for a seller to withhold until after the signing certain information that a buyer will want to review, such as the seller's list of customers.

PROVIDING CUSTOMER NAMES AND PERMITTING CONTACTS WITH THEM. The most valued asset of many companies is its list of customers. At the same time, most buyers will want to review the customer list prior to the closing. From a seller's perspective, providing the customer list is one of the last things that should be done prior to the closing, especially if a competitor is purchasing the company.

Most buyers not only will want the list of customers but also will want to contact key customers to verify their continued satisfaction with the company being sold. It is usually wise to get an agreement between the buyer and seller as to which customers will be contacted. Then, the seller will usually want to call the designated customers in advance and tell them about his plans to sell the company and about the forthcoming call from the buyer.

If any contacts are to be made in person by the buyer, it is often worthwhile for the seller or one of his representatives to accompany the buyer on the visit. By sitting in on the conversations when the buyer talks to customers, the seller or his representative will usually have some influence on what is covered in the conversation and can minimize any negative comments that otherwise might be made by customers about the seller's business.

FACILITATING CONTACTS WITH EMPLOYEES. Another sensitive subject is communicating with employees about the pending sale, both by the seller and the buyer. The seller usually does not want to tell all of his employees that a sale is imminent until the definitive sale agreement and related documents have been signed and a target closing date has been selected. Prior to talking to his employees, he should anticipate as many potential questions as possible and prepare appropriate responses. Among the key questions that employees will have are: "What does the pending sale mean to me?"; "Will I still have the same job?"; "Will my responsibilities change?"; "Will my pay change?"; and "Will my benefit programs change?"

Usually it is wise for the buyer and seller to hold employee meetings jointly. The seller can begin by discussing the forthcoming sale in general and introduce the new owner or his representative(s). They, in turn, can then discuss plans they have for the business and its people after the closing. The purpose of this exercise is to minimize employee concerns and keep employees motivated to continue working hard for the business. (Of course, if the buyer plans to decimate the staff after the closing, he will probably have little need to try to motivate employees.)

In addition to general employee meetings, it is important for the buyer and seller to meet with each key member of management individually to discuss plans for him. If his position is not going to be maintained, his severance package should be discussed with him. When a seller does not want certain key employees to leave the business before the closing, it is often worth offering these individuals a financial incentive—a "stay bonus"—if they will remain through the closing. As discussed previously, I have found that stay bonuses can be a particularly good investment for a seller to motivate key employees to remain until the closing and also to help the seller operate his business well during the period prior to the closing.

In addition to general communications with employees, the buyer will usually want to do some due diligence on employees between the signing and the closing. This is the time when the buyer customarily decides which of the management people it will retain and how positions will be altered or combined to create the organizational structure with which it will operate. Such decisions will involve getting to know each manager: his strengths, weaknesses, and personality. Some of this information will come from one-on-one meetings, while other insights will emerge as the buyer talks to other managers and works with each individual manager as it gets to know the business better and completes its due diligence.

UNDERTAKING A MID-YEAR AUDIT. To many companies, particularly those that are publicly traded, it is very important that businesses they purchase be audited by a well-respected accounting firm to ensure that all financial statements conform to generally accepted accounting principles. This is especially important to public companies, because in the future the financial results of the acquired business will be integrated into the buyer's own public financial statements, and the buyer will want to minimize any surprising adjustments that an acquisition might cause.

If a respected firm has regularly audited the business being sold, its audits will usually be acceptable to a buyer (although recently, the lack of proper audits by some well-known accounting firms may result in tighter scrutiny of medium and smaller-sized firms as well as large companies). In cases where the seller's audits are to be used, the buyer typically has its own public accounting firm go over the audit work papers and discuss them with the public accounting firm that prepared them. The buyer may also want its audit team to roll forward the most recent audit to the closing date, which will effectively bring the audit up-to-date and minimize surprises between the last formal audit and the closing date.

If the transaction involves a sale of stock rather than assets and if the company being sold has not been formally audited or has been audited only by a local firm, a buyer will sometimes request the right to have its public accounting firm perform an audit prior to the closing. This will usually involve taking a formal inventory of all assets, as well as computing the value of all current assets and liabilities the company has. Generally the cost of such an audit is borne by the buyer, but the seller will need to make his financial team available to the buyer's audit team during the process, so both parties probably will incur costs in this process.

REVIEWING PAST TAX RETURNS. A buyer typically will want to have its financial team review the selling company's tax returns for the past three to five years. This will be particularly important if the sale is for the stock of the company rather than for its assets. In a stock sale, even though a buyer of stock may get a strong representation and indemnity from the seller for any unpaid taxes, governmental tax authorities will still look to the buyer (as owner of the stock of the company) for payment of any back taxes.

When assets rather than stock are sold and the seller retains control of the stock, tax authorities will usually look initially to the seller for any unpaid taxes. In some circumstances, however, they may still come after the buyer of the assets for unpaid claims if the seller has dissolved the corporation he sold and does not have the financial resources to pay the taxes. Then, a lien might be attached to the assets that were purchased in the sale. So, whether purchasing stock or assets, it is important for a buyer to satisfy itself that any and all past taxes owed have been paid.

ROLE OF THE BUYER IN INTERIM DECISIONS. As previously mentioned, the definitive sale agreement may provide certain roles for the buyer in the decision-making process between the signing and the closing. For example, usually the sale agreement will specify a dollar amount above which all contracts, leases, fixed asset commitments, or other agreements will require the approval of the buyer. In addition, compensation increases above a certain percentage or dollar amount are likely to require the buyer's approval.

The seller also will usually want to keep the buyer posted or invite input on other key decisions that he is considering, such as opportunities to provide incentives to attract new customers, even though the buyer's formal approval is not required under the sale agreement. This enables the buyer to be involved in important decisions before he takes over and enhances the probability of a smooth transition after the closing.

I have seen a case in which a seller did things to make the transition period difficult for the buyer, including making numerous large dollar commitments (such as across-the-board salary increases as big as permitted under the sale agreement), all without contacting the buyer prior to making the commitments. To this day I do not understand the motivation for this conduct—especially since the seller was getting an extremely attractive price for his business—other than providing his employees with a farewell present at the buyer's expense. Such conduct may cause employees to remain loyal to the former owner and make it more difficult for the buyer to gain their support. It behooves a buyer to make sure that the definitive sale agreement provides adequate controls over the seller's actions in the conduct of the business between the signing and the closing.

CLOSING THE TRANSACTION

PREPARING A CLOSING DATE BALANCE SHEET. As previously discussed, the value of the assets and liabilities of a business will change between the time the purchase price is originally established and the closing. Therefore, it is customary just before the closing for the seller to prepare a closing date balance sheet to determine an adjusted purchase price to be paid at the closing. Usually the buyer's financial people will have the right to participate in this process.

The balance sheet prepared just before the closing may be the one used to determine the final purchase price, with no post-closing purchase adjustment. In this case, the inventory usually will be taken over the weekend prior to the closing, receivables and payables will be totaled during the same weekend, and a final valuation will be agreed to prior to a Monday closing. As previously mentioned, the advantage to the seller of preparing the closing date balance sheet right before the closing and making it the basis for computing the final purchase price is that the seller is still in control of the company's financial people, who will determine most of the values.

After the closing, employee loyalties can be expected to shift to the buyer. Thus, the seller can expect to be at some disadvantage if the purchase price used at the closing is based on projected balance sheet amounts and the final balance sheet is to be prepared after the closing. A final balance sheet prepared after the closing gives the buyer an opportunity to work with the employees to raise issues that could reduce valuations to the detriment of the seller.

PREPARING FOR THE TRANSFER OF FUNDS. During the week before the closing, the buyer and seller should make arrangements for the transfer of funds at the closing—if part or all of the purchase price is to be paid in cash. Usually the simplest way for the buyer to pay the seller cash is through a wire transfer. The buyer will need to accumulate adequate funds in a particular account immediately prior to the closing, and the seller will need to provide the buyer with information about his account and bank wire number prior to the transfer of funds. If this is all done a day or two in advance of the closing, it facilitates an easy transfer.

The buyer and seller should also verify the latest time of day to initiate a wire transfer that will get good funds credited to the seller's account so he will earn interest for the day. The buyer and seller also have to factor in the impact of different time zones if one bank is located in a different time zone than the other.

It is important to schedule the start of the closing so there will be adequate time to review and sign all documents before the wire transfer needs to be initiated. Depending on the complexity of the transaction, a closing can take several hours. Consequently, it is highly desirable for the attorneys for the buyer and the seller to have reviewed all documents (including their respective written opinions to each other) during the week before the closing. One of the attorneys should also prepare a schedule of all documents to be signed at the closing and have the other party's attorney make sure in advance of the closing that he agrees with the document agenda.

Once all documents have been signed at the closing, the buyer should place a phone call to its bank to initiate the wire transfer to the seller's bank account. About an hour or so after the wire transfer has been requested, the buyer's bank should be able to provide a Federal Reserve wire transfer number. This should be given to the seller's bank so it can watch for the specific wire transfer. Once the seller's bank acknowledges receipt of the wired funds, the transaction is completed and copies of final documents can be exchanged.

Despite good planning for the closing and the transfer of funds, things can happen that complicate the execution of a smooth closing. Sometimes unexpected issues are raised at the closing by one of the sides and require time for resolution. Occasionally, the attorneys decide another document needs to be prepared, which then requires time for drafting and subsequent review by the other side. And sometimes one of the signators is late to the closing and that imposes further delays. To minimize the problem of getting timely signatures and to save time at the closing, attorneys will often have their clients sign many of the documents prior to the closing and then hold the documents until the closing.

While most closings usually run smoothly and funds are transferred with time to spare, some do drag on much longer than expected. When it seems that there is a chance the closing will run past the wire transfer deadline and even past normal banking hours, the buyer should make arrangements with his bank to have an authorized bank employee remain on duty to receive the request for a wire transfer for the following day. Alternatively, the buyer may decide to give the seller a check for the purchase price because it is too late to initiate a wire transfer. In that case, the seller should make provision for safeguarding the check overnight and getting it deposited when the bank opens the following morning.

While I have had closings delayed several hours because of problems that arose during the closing procedures, I have never had one go into the following day. I have had them run past the time that wire transfers could be initiated, past the time the banks closed, and past the time when a bank employee would stay on duty. I even had one that did not get completed until just before midnight, but it was still the same day.

The best way to minimize the possibility that a closing will last longer than a few hours is good planning by the attorneys for both sides, including agreeing on the agenda of documents to be signed and exchanged, reviewing all documents in advance, getting all documents that require third-party signatures (such as lease transfer consents) signed in advance, and making arrangements in advance for transferring funds. Such planning will greatly reduce the time required—and the potential level of frustration—at the closing.

CHAPTER THIRTEEN

LIFE AFTER THE CLOSING

The closing is now over, the transaction has been completed, and the seller has his proceeds. The process of selling a business is over for the seller, but a few things may still remain to be done, especially if the seller has agreed to stay on for a transition period—even if only in a consulting capacity—or if the transaction involves an earn-out period. In addition, most sellers will need to make provisions for re-investing the proceeds from the sale of their business. And, finally, every seller needs to address what he wants to do in the next phase of his life. This chapter addresses each of these issues.

HELPING THE NEW OWNER AFTER THE CLOSING

If the seller founded the business or owned it for an extended period, he probably will have earned the loyalty of the company's employees and its customers. When the seller has earned such loyalty, he can be of considerable assistance to the new owner during the transitional period of ownership. For example, the seller can provide the new owner with insights about key customers. If they did not call on key customers together during the due diligence period prior to the closing, the new owner may want the seller to join him on selected calls to explain the transition.

One of the most important—and among the most difficult—adjustments that a seller needs to make is to accept the fact that, even though he may be retained to head the business through a transition period, he is no longer the ultimate decision-maker. He now has to answer to someone in the buyer's organization. An even greater change occurs if the seller is only to serve as a consultant after the closing. In this case, he is no longer the ultimate decision-maker, and will usually only be called on for advice on selected issues.

A seller needs to be able to accept the reality of his new position after the closing. In most cases, he will work only part-time at his former company. He can still be an effective contributor and sounding board for the new owner, but he needs to recognize that the company can no longer have the same importance in his life as it did before. If he maintains a good relationship with the buyer, he can provide meaningful counsel to the buyer on a variety of issues, but that is all it is: counsel, not decision-making.

Many former owners become frustrated watching a new owner manage their former business. They see decisions being made with which they disagree. They may even see the business mismanaged and sales turn down. Watching from the sidelines after being on the playing field for a long time—able to make good plays—is a difficult adjustment to make. But, again, if the seller has only been retained to be a consultant, all he can do is try to provide effective counsel to the new owner.

OPERATING THE BUSINESS
DURING AN EARN-OUT PERIOD

In those situations in which part of the purchase price is to be paid in the form of an earn-out, the seller may be more involved in the business after the closing. In some instances, the buyer will agree to have the former owner stay on and run the business during the earn-out period. Even if the former owner is not actively involved in the day-to-day decision-making process, he still needs to stay close enough to the business to make sure that the business is operated in such a manner as to not adversely affect profits (and his payout) during the earn-out period.

Ideally, the seller and the buyer will operate the business on a partnership basis during an earn-out period. The ability to do this will usually be enhanced if the buyer and seller agree prior to the closing on the basic guidelines that will be pursued in managing the business during the earn-out period. It also helps if they develop an operating budget for the earn-out period.

Of uppermost importance in developing an operating budget is to reach agreement on the expense level that will be used, so the new owner does not try to load up the business with expenses to enhance long-term sales at the cost of reducing short-term profits during the earn-out period. The buyer and the seller need to agree on how much investment spending will be done during the earn-out period to enhance long-term growth, and adjust the earnings targets accordingly. Then, if the buyer subsequently decides to make an acquisition or further increase other investment spending to expand the business faster, earnings targets need to be further adjusted so the seller is not penalized with a lower payout during the earn-out period.

I have seen some earn-outs work extremely well and others not work well at all. I believe that, more than anything else, success depends on the ability of the buyer and the seller to reach a solid understanding prior to the closing about how the business will operate after the closing.

As I mentioned previously, one of the most successful earn-outs with which I have been associated was a food distribution business that was acquired by another food company. The two brothers who were selling the distribution business had developed a plan of action for expanding the business. The sellers retained their management positions during the earn-out period and operated the business with great autonomy, but they kept the new owner closely apprised of all key decisions. A close working relationship developed. The new owner served as a sounding board to the sellers and reserved the right to make all critical decisions. But the sellers continued to run the business as though they were still the owners.

The pre-closing agreement called for the sellers to deduct the cost of borrowing funds from the parent company from the earnings used to calculate the earn-out, so any investment spending for growth had to increase earnings enough to cover the cost of capital. At the end of the three-year period, the sellers received all of the earn-out money available to them. It had been a very successful financial experience for both the sellers and the buyer, so the sellers continued to operate the business for a few years after the earn-out period ended. That they stayed on after it ended is, I believe, the ultimate indicator that both parties felt good about the relationship they developed during the earn-out period.

INVESTING THE SALE PROCEEDS

One of the most important decisions that a seller has to make after the closing is how to invest the proceeds received from the sale of his business. In many instances, the seller will have more cash in his control than he has ever had previously, and he needs to make sound decisions on what to do with it.

The seller should consult with his tax advisor early in the selling process to examine the potential effects of alternative structures (such as a sale of stock versus a sale of assets) on the after-tax proceeds of the projected selling price. Good tax counsel can be extremely valuable to a seller, enabling him to retain as much in after-tax proceeds as possible. The key here is to try to get as much of the selling price as possible treated as capital gains, rather than ordinary income, to take advantage of a substantially lower tax rate.

The next step is to find a competent investment advisor. The investment advisor should begin by helping the seller determine the most appropriate allocation for investing the proceeds. Other investments the seller may have made, his age, and his other financial responsibilities are all factors to be weighed in the investment allocation decision, as are such issues as whether the seller wants to purchase another business or to pay down outstanding debt in other investments with part of the proceeds.

Assuming there will still be a substantial amount available to reinvest after taxes and other financial commitments are paid, a seller and his investment advisor need to consider how much liquidity the seller should have in his investments. If the seller intends to purchase a second home or make another major purchase near-term, then sufficient funds need to be set aside in a fairly liquid form so cash will be readily available for those purposes. Obviously, a seller does not want to put all of his proceeds in stocks and/or long-term bonds when he may need a significant amount of cash to purchase a second home in 6 to 12 months; the market value of stocks and bonds could be down significantly when the seller needs to raise cash to close on his new home.

Once short-term needs have been provided for, the seller should decide how to allocate funds to be placed in long-term investments. An investment advisor may recommend that an older-aged seller place a greater portion of his portfolio in bonds and other conservative investments. Not only do the prices of bonds tend to fluctuate less than stocks, but most have a higher yield, thus providing more current income. To a seller who is in his late 60s, for example, having less value fluctuation and a higher current yield is often more important than the fact that over the longer term stocks generally provide a higher overall return because of greater capital gains.

Real estate investment—such as buying a commercial building, a small office building, an apartment building, or farmland—may also be appropriate for part of a seller's portfolio. Professional managers can be retained to oversee each of these types of real estate to minimize the owner needing to be involved in their ongoing operation.

If the seller takes part or all of his proceeds in the stock of the publicly traded company that bought his business, other factors need to be considered. The seller and his investment advisor need to develop a plan outlining what portion, if any, of this stock should become a permanent part of the seller's investment portfolio. Diversification is important for all investors, as has been seen in recent years when numerous employees lost most of their 401(k) investments in their company's stock—and in some instances all of it. Even highly regarded companies can have declines in earnings that send the value of their shares skidding downward.

So, a seller should generally have a plan to sell off a portion of the stock he receives if that constitutes a significant portion of the value of his overall estate. How quickly he sells off part or all of the stock will depend on several factors. First, what restrictions have the buyer and SEC regulations placed on how soon the stock can be sold after a closing? If the stock is not registered, it needs to be registered prior to any market sale. If the stock is already registered, it can usually be sold within six months after a sale.

Second, the seller and his investment advisor will want to weigh the outlook for the company whose stock the seller has received. If the outlook for future earnings is bright, obviously there is less urgency to sell than if the long-term outlook is not as good, or if the stock is trading at a near-record price and now appears to be a good time to lock up an attractive price.

Third, one needs to take into consideration overall market conditions, including the current state of the economy and its outlook for the coming year. If stock prices are generally at the upper end of the normal trading range for price-earnings multiples, then it probably would be wise to lock up a good price now rather than wait. Likewise, if the economy is strong at the moment but there is uncertainty about how long it will remain so, that may also be an indicator to cash in some of the stock received in the sale proceeds.

Finally, a seller must weigh the tax implications of his investment decisions. When the seller receives stock as payment for the sale of his company, capital gains tax liability usually is postponed until that stock is sold. Thus, any plan to sell stock received from a sale needs to factor in payment of capital gains taxes. And, in any plan for allocating the re-investment of cash received from the sale of the business—or subsequent sale of stock received in the sale of the business—the tax implications of the new investments should be assessed and weighed before making final investment decisions.

Generally, it is beneficial to delay paying taxes as long as possible so that one has more money to invest and grow. Likewise, it usually is preferable to try to have as much income as possible taxed at capital gains rates rather than at higher ordinary income tax rates. There are, of course, exceptions to these generalities, and that is why a seller should retain good tax and investment advisors before he makes key decisions about how to re-invest the proceeds received from the sale.

DECIDING ON THE NEXT STEPS IN YOUR LIFE

Often a key motivation when a business owner decides to sell his company is a strong desire to do something other than continue to run his business. If this is the case, he may have a well-thought-out plan for what he will do after the closing. For example, one of my clients had a carefully considered 12-year plan of activities that he wanted to pursue after the closing. He was 68 years old when he retained me to sell his company, and he wanted to complete his plan by age 80.

Other sellers may have a general idea of what they want to do but no specific plans. Another client of mine planned to build a home in Florida and play golf, but had no plans beyond that. A third client planned to start a new business sometime after the closing but had no specific plans for it. But, many owners sell their businesses without any real notion of what they want to do next. They may decide that the market opportunity is right for them to sell, proceed with a sale, and wait until after the closing before determining what to do in the future.

If a seller has not done so earlier, one of the first things he should do after the closing (or after completing any full-time service to the business he agreed to perform following the closing) is to develop a plan for the next phase of his life. The following list of questions is an example of some of the issues that a seller might wish to consider in the process of deciding what comes next.

1. Do I want to retire or to continue working?

2. If I do not want to retire yet, what kind of work do I want to do?

   - Do I want to own another business?

   - If so, do I want to buy one or start a new one? If I decide to buy another company or start a new one, how will I answer the following:

     - On what products or services do I wish to focus?

     - If I seek to purchase a business, how do I find the right company?

     - What resources will I need if I plan to start a new company?

- ◆ How big do I want the company to become?

- If I do not want to own another company but still want to work, what line of work would I enjoy?

  - ◆ For example, would I like to be an industry consultant, with flexible hours and working conditions? (Part of the answer to this question may be whether the seller wants to work on his own or for another firm.)

  - ◆ Would I like to work in an entirely different field, such as taking an appointed position in federal, state, or local government—or perhaps even run for political office?

  - ◆ Would I like to work in the non-profit field (such as for a church, synagogue, or service organization), perhaps having a full-time position but with lower compensation than I previously earned? Would I rather work part-time than full-time?

3. If am ready to retire, what do I want to do and where do I want to do it?

   - Would I like to perform volunteer service on a part-time basis? If so, how many hours a week would I like to contribute and what type of work would I enjoy?

   - How much flexibility do I want with my time? For example, how much travel would I like to do and where would I like to travel?

   - Do I want to relocate my home, either on a permanent or seasonal basis?

   - If I move to a new seasonal or permanent home, what location would I prefer?

If you do not know where you want to relocate yet, consider renting for a month at a time in different locations—long enough to give you an opportunity to get to know a place but short enough so you do not feel tied down too long if you do not enjoy it after getting a good flavor of the area.

To illustrate the importance of thinking through such issues, let me tell you about two different couples who are friends of mine. A few years ago, the first couple purchased a lot on which to build a seasonal home in the mountains in Colorado. From their description, it is a beautiful lot overlooking a river at the bottom of a canyon with mountains in the background. Now they are about ready to retire and begin building their mountain dream home.

In recent discussions with his wife, the husband learned that she hoped they would stay in their new mountain home five or six months each year, while he had assumed they would stay there for only about three months during the summer, and then spend the rest of the year at their other planned home in Arizona. They both love to play golf and hope to play at least three times a week. When I asked how close their Colorado lot was to the golf courses where they would play, the husband responded that they would have about a 45-minute drive each way. I asked if such a long drive three or four times a week would diminish the fun of playing a round of golf, resulting in less frequent play. He replied that he had not thought about that.

Given such potentially significant issues, I suggested that, before starting on their new home, they consider renting a condo for a month near where they planned to build. Then, they could drive to the golf courses they wanted to play three to four times a week and see how they adjusted to the remoteness of their building site. The husband readily agreed that was something they needed to do before starting construction—and that it might also help them resolve their differences on how much time each year they would want to live in Colorado versus the other home they planned to have in Arizona.

These friends are in contrast to a couple of other good friends. For years they had lived in New Jersey, where he commuted to work in Manhattan and she had an excellent position with a company near their home. When both retired in their early 60s, they decided to relocate to the mountains of North Carolina. They made this decision after spending time in the area and looking at alternative options. After considerable reflection, they purchased an attractive freestanding home on a golf course in the mountains near Asheville. Both are avid golfers, and living on the golf course allows them to play at least four times a week, making the two-minute drive to the clubhouse in their own golf cart.

Their research had also led them to realize that because this was a new community, all the residents were new to the area and were openly seeking new friendships just as they were. After a few months of getting to know the other people in the development, both through playing golf and participating in various other interest groups, they felt right at home. Making their decision after considerable research, planning, and reflection significantly enhanced the probability of their moving to a new place where they could develop a genuine feeling of happiness.

The thought that I want to leave you with is that whatever a seller decides to do after the sale of his business, he will probably be more content with that decision if he gives it considerable thought before he commits to it. If you have not done so before the closing, take time after the closing for a period of real reflection on what you want to do next and where you want to do it. After spending years owning and managing a business, an owner has earned the right to take at least a couple of months to focus on these key issues. Reflection and thoughtful planning will enhance the probability that you will enjoy the next phase of your life more than if you just stumble into it without a lot of forethought.

CHAPTER FOURTEEN

EPILOGUE— LESSONS LEARNED FROM PERSONAL NEGOTIATIONS

Over nearly three decades of successfully negotiating the purchase and sale of more than 100 businesses, I have had lots of interesting experiences. I would like to share a few, and the key lessons I learned from them.

LESSON ONE: HOLD FIRM ON INITIAL TERMS OF AGREEMENT AND AVOID EXCESSIVE EMOTION DURING NEGOTIATIONS

When a buyer makes an offer to pay a fixed price for a business, do not get talked into lowering that price unless the condition of the business or its assets have deteriorated since the time the offer was made. At the same time, excessive emotion in negotiations is usually not rewarded. I think the following story illustrates both these points well.

Several years ago I was representing my company in seeking to sell seven grain elevators located on the Mississippi and Illinois rivers. We had held an auction (which I coordinated) among the large grain companies, and the winning bid was some 30 percent higher than the second-highest bid. The highest bidder was one of the large international grain companies, and I learned later that its CEO had told his Senior Vice President for North American Grain Operations to do whatever was necessary to be the winning bidder, as the elevators we were selling would nicely complement their existing river elevator network. But, I think the CEO also made it clear to his senior officer to try to reduce the original bid during subsequent negotiations. This set the stage for prolonged and tense negotiations.

Our first face-to-face meeting with the buyer was in Chicago. Two outside lawyers and I represented the selling company. The buyer was represented by its Senior Vice President for North American Grain Operations, one of his key lieutenants, and one of his senior engineers. The engineer had just led a small group from the buyer on a due diligence tour of the seven grain elevators that were for sale. The buyer's purpose in our initial meeting was to itemize a long list of concerns it had found during its tour, with the overall objective of trying to substantially reduce its bid.

After the engineer finished discussing his extensive list of problems, their team waited for my response. I sat quietly, saying nothing for an extended period. The silence became deafening. Finally, in a hushed voice, I slowly stated that the price was still the same, explaining that everyone knew that these were not new elevators and that they were being sold in "as is, where is" condition.

I went on to state that the numerous flaws that had been recited were due to ordinary wear and tear, which would be expected to occur over the many years the elevators had been in use. I further indicated that we were fully willing to enter into a formal agreement to sell the elevators for the price they had bid, but if they were now only willing to purchase them at a reduced price, we would move on to have discussions with the next highest bidder (knowing all along that we did not want to have to do that for fear of having to take the sharply lower price that bidder had offered).

It took the group on the other side of the table a while to regain its composure after I finished. In a few sentences, I had completely dismissed their carefully laid rationale for getting a price reduction. In the end, the only accommodation that I made to them in terms of a price reduction was recognizing that a crack in the seawall at one of our elevators needed to be repaired, and so offered to reduce the price by the cost of that repair. This was damage that we had not previously known about, and that we would have had to repair if we retained the elevators.

My response to their efforts to get a price reduction set the stage for the ensuing negotiations. Repeatedly, the buyer tried in all kinds of ways to upstage the negotiations and to seek preferential terms. But, because we steadfastly maintained our position, the buyer was quite unsuccessful in enhancing its position from the original terms submitted. I know that the inability of the other team's lead negotiator to get more favorable terms drove him up the wall.

On one noteworthy occasion, we were engrossed in trying to work out an issue. I made what I thought was a logical defense of our side's position. The second person on the other side was moved to say that he felt our position, as I had articulated it, sounded reasonable to him. When the lead negotiator heard that from his associate, he snapped. He picked up the chair next to him and physically hurled it across the table to the other side of the room and screamed to his associate that if he was going to agree with us, he should go and sit on the same side of the table with our team. This emotional outburst did not enhance his negotiating position. In fact, it signaled desperation rather than strength in his demands.

After several days of protracted negotiations, our team decided that we had been through enough. We had tried to bargain in good faith, but the leader of the other side never felt he got enough. Thus, when we walked into the negotiating room on the morning that both sides had previously selected as the target day to complete the transaction, I told the other team that we had checked out of our hotel and brought our bags to the meeting. I explained that, if the transaction was not completed in time for funds to be wire-transferred yet that day, we would leave, contact the next highest bidder, and immediately start negotiations with that party.

All day long we continued to negotiate in good faith, but reminded our opponents that the clock was running and that we were serious about leaving if they had not initiated a wire transfer of funds to our account by 3:00 P.M., which was the latest that a wire could be initiated and still have the funds credited to our account that day. At 2:00 P.M., they were still arguing, going over and over the same issues they had wanted us to give in on. We kept reminding them about the lateness of the hour. During the last hour they tried everything to get more concessions. We remained unmoved, because the concessions they were seeking were not in the spirit of the terms originally agreed to.

Finally, at about 2:58 P.M. they concluded that we were serious about leaving and that they had gotten all they were going to, so they called their bank and initiated the wire transfer. We had always sought to negotiate in good faith and seek middle ground wherever possible, but when they tried to go past what we felt was reasonable and beyond the original intent of the contemplated transaction, we had to show them that we were fully prepared to walk. Once they saw this, they took the necessary steps to complete the transaction.

The moral of this story is the importance of holding to the terms that were originally proposed and being willing to walk before agreeing to a fundamental change in price or other key terms. Also, never let excessive emotion disrupt the tenor of the negotiations.

Lesson Two: Be Willing to Stand Up to an Opposing Attorney

Sometimes a buyer or seller will retain a high-powered, well-known attorney who thinks he can run over you in negotiations. When this occurs, you need to be fair and courteous but stand your ground. Above all, do not let him continually call all the shots. The next story describes the process my associates and I used to deal with such a situation.

In this series of negotiations, I was representing the company I worked for on the purchase of a majority position in a publicly traded seed corn company. Again, I was working with the same two lawyers for our firm whom I had worked with on the sale of the river elevators. The founder of the seed corn company controlled a majority of the company's outstanding shares, and we were seeking to purchase these from him and his family. We had reached general agreement with him on the purchase terms during an extended meeting in the basement of his home in a small midwestern community.

Once we had reached agreement with the owner, he decided to hire a nationally-known attorney. Together, the owner and his new attorney decided to see how much they could further sweeten the deal for the sellers. Our team had extensive negotiations with the attorney over the phone. One Friday I got the seller and his attorney on the phone together; they promised me that there were only two remaining issues to negotiate—which they identified. I was further told that if our team would fly out to the attorney's office the following Monday morning, he would work diligently with us to resolve those two issues that day.

Early Monday morning our team flew to meet with the attorney. When we arrived at his office, we were greeted by his secretary who told us that he was in court that morning but had prepared a memo for us to review. We were shocked to see that, rather than just two issues, the attorney's memo listed 54(!) issues of disagreement with our draft of the purchase agreement.

We carefully reviewed the memo and prepared our response. Around noon the attorney returned and sometime later his client arrived. We sat in the attorney's conference room and negotiated non-stop until after midnight, never leaving the room nor taking a break except to go to the restroom. Finally, at 12:30 A.M.—after our team had spent over 15 solid hours in the conference room—we completed our negotiations and reached agreement on all terms in the purchase agreement, or so we were told. Needless to say, we were not prepared to stay overnight, as we had brought no clothing or toiletries. But we checked into a motel, got a little sleep, and then flew home the next morning.

When the attorney got our draft of the purchase agreement with the revisions that he had said he agreed to during our marathon session, he called and said he had several further changes that he wanted to make in the purchase agreement. We were shocked, but responded that, if they could not be resolved over the phone, he was going to have to fly out and meet with us in our offices. He reluctantly agreed. Several days later he came to our offices about noon. We spent all afternoon refining the agreement, having a secretary retype each page as we completed changes on it.

As time for his evening flight approached, we told the attorney that before he left we wanted him to physically sign off on the document before he got on his plane. We all got in my car and handed him the purchase agreement and told him to initial each page so that he could not come back yet another time with more changes. I then drove a very circuitous route to the airport, taking much longer than normal, so that he could read and initial every page (about 65 as I recall) before our attorneys and I let him off at the airport.

We hated to be so demanding, but we knew of no other way to handle him (or his client), as we were sure that the attorney would keep requesting further changes on behalf of his client and keep delaying the closing. As it turned out, our tactic worked, and, having initialed each page, the attorney made no further requests for changes. We proceeded to get the purchase agreement signed and the transaction closed without further major hitches.

We stood up to a famous attorney, and he ultimately went along.

LESSON THREE: PERSISTENCE USUALLY PAYS

I have always believed that one of the most important personal assets in buying or selling a business is persistence. I never found persistence more necessary—nor received a more successful result from being persistent—than I did in the following story.

During the time I was the vice president of corporate planning and development for a large food company, we developed a strategy to try to build a leading position in manufacturing branded products (preferably frozen) for the foodservice market. We identified a few companies that exemplified types of the firms we would like to purchase. One of those that we had a particular interest in became available when its parent company was acquired by a financial investor who decided to seek buyers for the part of the acquired company that made branded food products.

The business in which we were interested was a leading marketer of frozen breaded-and-battered appetizers sold to restaurants. The company seeking to divest it also had a second frozen foodservice company, one of the leading marketers of frozen Mexican foodservice products. We decided to bid for both of these businesses.

(Before I go further, I should mention that until about a year earlier I had been a corporate officer of the firm now seeking to sell these businesses, so I knew both businesses quite well. In fact, I had been heavily involved in the negotiations to purchase the Mexican foodservice business. The ensuing takeover of my former company and the decision to sell its branded food businesses, however, all took place several months after I left that company and joined the second firm.)

The bidding process started during the summer, and was coordinated by the seller's investment banking firm. I knew the key person coordinating the sale at the large Wall Street firm, having worked with him while I was an officer of my old firm. I did not, however, know the people who had purchased my former company and who were now seeking to sell its branded food businesses. Their headquarters was in suburban Los Angeles, so when I was vacationing in Southern California with my family that August, I made an appointment to meet the acquiring firm's officer in charge of corporate development.

While my family waited outside, I spent about an hour with the new owner's corporate development guru. I summarized my new company's strategy for expanding into frozen foodservice products and explained why we felt that both foodservice companies his firm was selling would fit well with our strategy. I also wanted to personalize our interest—let him get to know me (and display a little of my extensive knowledge of both these companies), and also get to know him personally and try to learn more about his company's strategy.

During the course of our discussion, I asked my counterpart whether price would be the sole determinant in selecting the firm to sell to, or whether they might also give consideration to what a buyer would do with the people in the acquired business. He responded that, while price was certainly going to be very important, they were interested in what the acquiring firm would do with the employees at the divisional level, as well as in the plants.

I explained why I felt we were somewhat unique in needing to get good divisional management as well as wanting to keep all the plants and the people who worked in them. I further explained that would not be the case with firms already in the foodservice business who were hoping to fold these operations into their current organizations. Since I knew that one of our main competitors was also in the frozen appetizer business, I indicated that some of the buyers would probably be looking at consolidating plants to gain efficiencies, and that many of the newly-acquired employees might face almost immediate termination.

In response to the case I made for my firm being a good firm for the employees of the two foodservice companies being sold, the seller's corporate officer made me a promise that was to become critical three months later. He promised me that, if our firm was within $2 million of the highest bidder for the two companies and we were deemed to be the preferred home for the employees of the businesses being sold, we would get the nod. But, if our bid was more than $2 million under the highest bid, they would go with the highest bidder regardless of its plans for the employees. With a handshake on that commitment, we parted.

Over the next several weeks we continued our review and evaluation process on both businesses. Our team concluded that the frozen appetizer business was a real gem and that, while the Mexican food company had some problems that would have to be resolved, it would fit our strategy and we should be open to purchasing it if we got it for an attractive price. In early October we put in a preliminary bid with a rather broad range in order to enhance our acceptance into the next round. We were subsequently accepted into the final round and proceeded to undertake extensive due diligence, including management meetings and plant visits.

As we prepared our final bids, our investment banker helped rationalize a little higher price for the appetizer business, so I felt we would be close to the needed price. The fact that we were willing to bid on both companies would, I knew, be deemed beneficial by the seller (they would have one less party to negotiate with compared to selling the two businesses to separate buyers).

We still had one more problem to overcome if we were to be the successful bidder. The seller needed to sell the stock of both companies rather than the assets, which we would have preferred purchasing. Our general counsel was adamant that we only buy assets. In fact, at a private lunch with our president, he stated that he would resign his position if the company went against him and offered to purchase the stock.

I knew that the selling company would have a much higher federal income tax liability if it sold assets instead of stock and, therefore, virtually any offer for assets would be rejected. I pleaded with our senior executives, promising them that if we were the winning bidder for stock we would not finalize the transaction unless they were satisfied that the seller was making sufficient representations and warranties, providing a solid indemnification, and placing adequate security behind the indemnification to properly protect us. I argued that we should be willing to purchase stock but should then seek protection that would make the transaction as comparable to an asset purchase as possible. Senior management agreed with me, and we submitted our bid for the stock of both foodservice companies.

Bids were due on a Friday in mid-November. I knew from making appropriate inquiries that the new owner of the selling company was going to meet with its investment banker the following Tuesday to discuss the bids and make a decision on which ones to select for the four companies being sold (there were two consumer food companies being sold in addition to the two frozen foodservice companies in which we were interested). I had also learned that the corporate development officer, with whom I had met in California three months earlier, was going to be in his company's apartment in New York City watching Monday Night Football the evening before the big meeting. Most important, I was able to obtain the telephone number at that apartment.

Right before the start of the football game, I called the corporate development officer and reminded him of his promise that, if our company was within $2 million of the highest bidder and we were still deemed to be the better home for the employees, they would give the nod to us. He readily acknowledged his memory of that and promised that he would keep his word. With that commitment, I knew we probably did not have to produce the highest bid, but just be within $2 million of it. I then went home, content that our team had done everything we could have reasonably done to optimize our chances of getting the nod.

About noon the next day, I got a call from the seller's investment banker stating that we were not the highest bidder for the two businesses, that in fact we were $3 million below the highest bidder. But, he quickly added that if we raised our bid by $1 million so that we were only $2 million under the highest bid, the seller was prepared to go with our firm because they felt we would be a better home for the employees.

At this point you may have assumed that our team said go ahead and give them the extra million and sew up the deal. It did not go like that. Instead, our top two officers felt the bankers and selling firm were playing a game just to get us to raise our bid another million. There was no way we could know for sure whether there really was another bidder $3 million higher than we were, and if not, whether they ultimately would take our original bid.

After much debate over two hours, I finally got approval to go the extra million. I ran back to my office and immediately dialed the investment banker. His secretary had to run to get him because he was getting on the phone with the higher bidder to give it the nod because we had taken longer than he had expected to give him a positive response. The investment banker broke off his effort to reach the other party and took my call, whereupon we reached oral agreement. In subsequent discussions with friends in the selling firm, I verified that in fact the highest bidder was $3 million over our bid, and that had we not raised our bid by that extra million we would have lost to the other party.

After getting the nod for both frozen food companies, one might think that the hardest part was over. As we were to learn, it was not. While numerous difficult issues came up in the process of negotiating the definitive purchase agreement, the most significant was getting tangible security behind the indemnification. If any of the representations or warranties made by the selling company were violated, we wanted to be able to collect the damages provided for in the purchase agreement.

But the selling company had been stripped of its liquid assets to help its new owner finance the original purchase. Moreover, the new owner of the selling company was not willing to join in the indemnification, so we would not have any tangible recourse unless we had specific assets on which we had a call. This was not purely academic, as the Mexican food company that we were seeking to acquire had some outstanding litigation with rather significant claims attached to the lawsuits. These claims would travel with the company; as the buyer of the stock, we would inherit the claims and become the ultimate payer of any finalized claims. With an asset sale, it would have been much more difficult to hold us liable for those claims.

During the negotiations, I flew to New York City for a meeting on getting our financial commitments in place. While I was there I arranged to meet with the Wall Street investment banker who was handling the sale and whom I had known when I worked at the selling company. We met at the Windows on the World restaurant atop one of the two 110-story towers of the World Trade Center (it is really difficult for me to accept the fact that they are no longer there). I laid out our case for needing appropriate security behind the indemnification.

The seller's investment banker responded that it was virtually unheard of for a selling firm to provide tangible security for an indemnification, and that the good faith and credit of this major corporation should be sufficient. I countered that the liquid assets of the selling company had already been stripped out by its new owner, and that a substantial amount of new debt had also been added to the selling company's books to help pay for the cost of the takeover by its new owner. I added that nothing could stop the new owner from carving out more assets to the point where the company selling us the two businesses might become a mere shell holding only illiquid assets.

After much discussion, the seller's investment banker inquired whether we might be willing to take a second mortgage on one of the selling firm's major facilities. I replied that we would need a sizeable amount of liquid assets, which we could draw on directly, ahead of any second mortgage. Ultimately, we got $10 million of liquid assets to which we had direct access and another $25 million in the form of a second mortgage on one of the selling company's largest plants, which had a market value well in excess of the combined amount of the first and second mortgages. Thankfully, we never had to draw on that security, but it was comforting to know that we had it if we ever needed to use it.

The process of negotiating the purchase agreement was exhausting. There were many days during which I was sure that we would not be successful, but I tried to focus on just the steps we had to take in a given day and not worry about the larger picture and all the items that had yet to be resolved. Taking the process one day at a time and breaking down the components into "bite-sized" pieces to be solved one at a time enabled us to get both transactions completed successfully.

Persistence really paid off.

LESSON FOUR: EVEN THE BEST NEGOTIATIONS DON'T ALWAYS SUCCEED

Usually persistence and good negotiating result in a successful outcome in either selling or buying a business. But sometimes factors which you cannot control are thrown into the process— and the ultimate result is disappointing. The following story dramatizes this.

Several years ago, I spent an enormous amount of time from September 30 to December 15 representing the company for which I worked in seeking to acquire the second largest broadline foodservice distributor in the country from a large, New York City-based international conglomerate. Had we been able to complete this acquisition it would have **tripled** the size of the company I worked for and permanently changed its direction. The story surrounding this proposed transaction is worth telling because it also illustrates the work involved in seeking to make acquisitions and divestitures.

Our CEO was firmly committed to seeking to shift the primary emphasis of the company from a food manufacturer to a foodservice distributor. He had overseen several acquisitions to expand our vending business—the nation's largest vending distributor. And we had recently completed the acquisition of a specialty foodservice distribution business, adding some $500 million in sales. Next, our CEO wanted to acquire a broadline distributor, but most of those he was considering were too small to be competitive against the likes of Sysco, the country's largest broadline distributor.

One Friday during this period, the **Wall Street Journal** had a story that a large leveraged buyout firm was in serious discussions to acquire the second largest broadline foodservice distribution business from its parent. I had repeatedly told our CEO that, if this particular broadline distributor ever became available, we should make a run for it. The reported selling price was around $700 million.

As soon as I saw the article, I suggested to our CEO that we throw our hat into the ring and become a second bidder for the business. After thinking about it for a couple of hours, he authorized me to call my counterpart at the large conglomerate and express our interest. When I called the executive, he was not available, so I faxed him a letter outlining my company's interest and requesting a meeting to discuss the subject further; I also left my office and home telephone numbers. I heard nothing back the rest of Friday or Saturday.

On Sunday evening I received a call at my home from a principal at the large conglomerate's investment banking firm, one of Wall Street's best known, who was acting as the large conglomerate's advisor in the negotiations on the sale of its foodservice distribution business. We had an extended phone conversation in which he queried me on the degree of our interest and our ability to pay in the area of three-quarters of a billion dollars for the foodservice distributor. I guess I whetted his interest enough so that on Monday we were invited by the large conglomerate to meet at its New York headquarters the following day. On Tuesday, October 4, our company's CFO and I flew to New York and met with some of the conglomerate's executives in one of its large, well-appointed conference rooms.

The meeting went well, and we were invited back to New York for two more days of meetings that week, Thursday and Friday, October 6 and 7. Thus, we made a hurried trip home on Tuesday afternoon, spent Wednesday getting ready for our next trip, and then were back in New York on Thursday and Friday. We signed a confidentiality agreement and spent the two days in New York getting extensive information on the distribution business. We were given the next few days to decide whether we wanted to proceed.

By the middle of the following week, we indicated to the large conglomerate that we were interested in proceeding, so we went back to New York at the end of that week. We spent the following Monday, October 17, getting ready for our fourth trip to New York on Tuesday and Wednesday. At this time we had to negotiate a letter of intent for the purchase of the distribution business; we also received more information on the business. The rest of the week was devoted to assessing that information and preparing for a trip the following week to the headquarters of the foodservice distribution company.

Several people from our company spent four days the next week (October 25–28) at the suburban Chicago headquarters of the distribution business. Even our CEO flew in to be a part of some of the meetings. The following Tuesday (November 1) we were back in Chicago, this time for meetings with our bankers. The following week we continued our due diligence work in our offices. On Friday, November 11, we had a special board of directors' meeting to share our findings and seek approval to proceed with our discussions; the board had numerous questions but felt that we should proceed.

The next week found us back in New York for four days of meetings with the large conglomerate (November 14–17). Things were heating up, and both sides were taking the discussions very seriously. During this time we hammered out a draft of the purchase agreement. I also was able to negotiate a significantly lower purchase price based on our due diligence to that date. When we left New York that Thursday evening, we had reached agreement on all of the major points, and the only real

open issue was our ability to get the necessary financial commitments from our banks. The next week was a shortened one due
to the Thanksgiving holidays.

When we returned to work the Monday after Thanksgiving,
November 28, we hosted an all-day meeting for our company's
major bankers to help them better understand the distribution
business we were seeking to purchase. Our senior executives
made comprehensive presentations on what the acquisition
would mean to our company. We also had an elaborate display
to show the breadth of the products that the distribution
business handled. The rest of the week was spent in discussions
with individual bankers and examining their financing
proposals.

The following Friday, December 9, we were back in New York
City, meeting with executives of the selling conglomerate and
its lawyers to finalize the definitive purchase agreement. We
obtained an agreement from the large conglomerate, but still
did not have our financing from the bankers. The bankers now
wanted the seller to hold some of the debt for the transaction,
something I knew would be difficult to convince the conglomerate to do. There were more discussions with our bankers the
first two days of the next week. By Wednesday, December 14,
the bankers reduced the amount of seller's paper that the
conglomerate would be required to accept as part of the transaction to $50 million, but they would not totally eliminate this
part of the financing.

I was sure that this was going to kill the deal, but I did my best
to try to persuade my counterpart at the conglomerate that same
afternoon that the proposed seller's paper was less than 10
percent of the transaction value, that the conglomerate would be
paid before any other holders of subordinate debt, and that I
was quite certain our firm was still offering a higher price than
the other bidder was (we knew that the selling conglomerate

had re-initiated discussions with the large leveraged buy-out firm it had originally talked to after it was evident we were having difficulty with our bankers).

The executives of the large conglomerate reflected on the proposal overnight, and my counterpart called me back the next morning (December 15), stating that his firm was unwilling to take any debt in the transaction and, therefore, any further efforts to finalize the proposed deal would have to be terminated. Later that day we reported the conglomerate's response to our board of directors as it gathered for its regular board meeting. Shortly thereafter, the conglomerate announced it had agreed to sell its foodservice distribution operation to the large leveraged buy-out firm, the original bidder, for a lower price than we had agreed to.

In the final analysis, our company was not able to complete the proposed transaction, and the original bidder still got the business (we did, however, force it to increase its price a reported $50 million over its original bid). While it was small consolation, our acquisition team had done an outstanding job of due diligence, taking a very complicated business and successfully dissecting the details behind each major functional area and operational activity. We uncovered information that even the conglomerate owner was not aware of and successfully used it to negotiate a multi-million-dollar reduction in the purchase price. And, we proved that we could go toe-to-toe against a first-rate New York team of corporate executives, investment bankers, and highly regarded lawyers.

We were, however, greatly disappointed in our bankers' inability to come up with adequate financing to complete the transaction, after their repeated promises early on that getting the financing would not be difficult. We never would have started down the road on this transaction had we not been assured by our bankers that they could raise the necessary money. It was, therefore, very disappointing that, when everyone else on our team had worked so hard and so successfully to make the transaction happen, our bankers let us down.

As evidenced by this story, not all negotiations have successful outcomes. In this case, however, the outcome was not caused by unsuccessful negotiating; rather, the banks did not deliver on their original promise, even though we re-negotiated the deal for a reduced price. While good negotiating does not always ensure you will reach your desired outcome, success in a transaction is unlikely to occur without good negotiating. And thorough preparations—coupled with good negotiating—will greatly enhance the likelihood of achieving success in any kind of business dealings.

*   *   *

I have written this book to help entrepreneurs prepare for and oversee the successful sale of a business. Hopefully, the book will help readers become more knowledgeable about and better equipped to sell a business. In the process, I also hope it enables them to receive better terms—both a higher price and better-crafted legal representations they make—than they would have before reading it. If that proves to be the case, this book has served its purpose.